THE TABERNACLE

THE TABERNACLE

JIMMY SWAGGART

JIMMY SWAGGART MINISTRIES
P.O. Box 262550 | Baton Rouge, Louisiana 70826-2550
Website: www.jsm.org | Email: info@jsm.org | Phone: 225.768.7000

ISBN 978-1-941403-02-0

09-125 | COPYRIGHT © 2014 Jimmy Swaggart Ministries®

15 16 17 18 19 20 21 22 23 / RRD / 11 10 9 8 7 6 5 4 3

TABLE OF CONTENTS

Introduction

Introduction

THE TABERNACLE, THE design of which was given to Moses directly by the Lord, presents one of the greatest studies in the entirety of the Word of God as it regards the person of Christ. Actually, every single part of the Tabernacle — its coverings, the way it was built, and its sacred vessels — all and without exception speak of Christ in either His atoning role, His mediatorial role, or His intercessory role. In other words, if you thoroughly study the Tabernacle, you will come out with a greater understanding of the Lord Jesus Christ than possibly you've ever had before.

THE SYMBOLS

In a sense, one might say that every single thing about the Tabernacle, and I mean everything, presents itself as a symbol of the work of our Lord. Consequently, if that is understood, then a greater understanding of Christ will be forthcoming as it regards your study of this all-important subject.

A PATTERN FOR LIVING

The Tabernacle was given by God to the Children of Israel to serve as a pattern for living. Nothing was left out. Nothing was excluded as it regards our lives. This study will show you how to live.

No, that doesn't mean that we are to go back and take upon ourselves the rudiments of the Tabernacle of old, for it has all been fulfilled in Christ, and I mean all was fulfilled. Paul said, *"For Christ is the end of the Law for righteousness to every-one who believes"* (Rom. 10:4). In essence, faith in Christ guar-antees the righteousness that the Law had but could not give.

THE TABERNACLE AND THE TEMPLE

When Paul wrote the book of Hebrews, and I believe that he did write that great book, the Holy Spirit had him to use the Tabernacle as an example of portraying Christ rather than the Temple. Considering how beautiful the Temple was, actually, the most costly building ever constructed in human history, why didn't the Lord have the apostle to use that great edifice?

The Temple basically portrayed the coming Kingdom Age when times will be a thousand percent different than now. The Tabernacle, however, portrayed the redemptive process greater than anything else, hence, the Holy Spirit using this as an example of Christ.

As you go down through the Tabernacle and understand somewhat about its functions, I think when you finish this perusal, you will know the Lord Jesus Christ to a greater degree than ever, and anything that will do that is valuable indeed!

1

The Tabernacle

CHAPTER ONE

The Tabernacle

*"AND THE **LORD** spoke unto Moses, saying"* (Ex. 25:1).

As we shall see, all of the specifications for the Tabernacle and its furniture were given by God to Moses. Moses was not given merely a plan but, in fact, a literal model to go by. So, it was all of God and none of man, as salvation is all of God and none of man.

Every design of the Tabernacle, the vessels, and all that pertained to it were actually representations of the heavenly. All were symbolic but pointed to the reality in Heaven.

As well, and even more important as it regards mankind, everything within and without the Tabernacle symbolized the person of the Lord Jesus Christ, who He was and what He did in order to redeem mankind.

Access to God is the lesson the Tabernacle and its vessels teach. I think anyone would agree that such a lesson is valuable indeed. The Tabernacle, therefore, is a manifestation of the glory of the grace of our Lord Jesus Christ and of His relationship with sinners who draw near unto Him.

THE STUDY

Concerning the study of the Tabernacle, which we are about to enter into, Arthur Pink said: *"We have now arrived at the longest, and most blessed, but least read and understood section of the great book of Exodus. From the beginning of Chapter 25 to the end of 40 — excepting the important parenthesis in 32/34 — the Holy Spirit has given us a detailed description of the Tabernacle, its structure, furniture, and priesthood."*

When we consider and understand that more space is devoted to the account of the Tabernacle than to any other single object or subject treated in Holy Writ, we then begin to understand its vast significance.

It took but two chapters to portray the record of God's work in creating this earth and fitting it for human habitation. By comparison, some 12 chapters were needed to tell us about the Tabernacle.

We make a vast mistake if we relegate the Tabernacle to ancient history, giving us only a record of Jewish manners and customs that have long since passed away, and which, we think, have no meaning for or value to us. But yet, the Word of God says: *"All Scripture is given by inspiration of God and is profitable"* (II Tim. 3:16). Pink said, and rightly so, *"The Christian cannot neglect any portion of the Word without suffering loss."*

Again and again in the New Testament, the Holy Spirit through the various writers makes figurative reference to the Tabernacle and its vessels. This means that much in the epistle to the Hebrews cannot be understood without reference to the contents of Exodus and Leviticus.

THE LORD JESUS CHRIST

The Tabernacle is actually a copy, one might say, of the original regarding that heavenly place in which God has His dwelling, but yet, in another sense, greatly different as it regards its simple form given on earth. To properly visualize the throne of God, we must inspect Revelation, Chapters 4 and 5. Only then can we catch a glimpse, and only a glimpse, of the glory and grandeur of the dwelling place of our Creator.

However, that which brings the Tabernacle home to the believer is the fact that its structure, its sacred furniture, its utensils, and, in fact, every single part of the Tabernacle, down to the lowliest pin that held the ropes in place, all and without exception, as stated, portrayed Christ in either His atoning, intercessory, mediatorial, or high priestly work. Actually, to fail to understand the Tabernacle is to fail to understand Christ. In beautiful type, symbolic and picture form, we see Christ represented in this structure, which helps us to understand who He is and what He did.

THE CROSS

As we study this structure as it presupposes Christ, we will find that the central theme is the Brazen Altar, which symbolizes the Cross of Christ where Jesus paid the price for man's redemption, taking the judgment of God upon Himself, all in our stead. Of course, in trying to evaluate the various pieces of sacred vessels, most would probably go to the Holy of Holies first of all. This housed the Ark of the Covenant, covered by the Mercy Seat, where God personally dwelt. But yet, let the

THE BRAZEN ALTAR

reader understand that this glorious destination of the Holy of Holies can never be reached unless one first goes by the way of the Brazen Altar, which typified the Cross of Christ. Today, as I sit here behind my desk holding this Dictaphone in my hand, knowing that my every sin has been washed away, and my name is written down in the Lamb's Book of Life, my heart swells with joy, knowing that I have eternal life. But yet, I also realize that it has come at such price — not a price that I had to pay, but a price that He paid!

So, what the Lord spoke to Moses some 3,500 years ago, we would do well to study, for the glories contained in that which the Lord gave to the great Lawgiver can never be exhausted. I only pray that in some small way, we can hopefully do a modicum of justice to the subject matter at hand. If so, as the Lord helps us, and if He reveals to you the significance of all of this which will be addressed, and I certainly believe He will to every searching heart, when your study is complete, closing out this great experience, I think you will have a greater picture of Christ than ever before, which the Tabernacle, in fact, is meant to portray.

THE OFFERING

"Speak unto the Children of Israel, that they bring Me an offering: of every man who gives it willingly with his heart you shall take My offering" (Ex. 25:2).

We find from this that God will have no gifts but such as are freely offered. He *"loves a cheerful giver."* If a man gives *"grudgingly or of necessity,"* God rejects the gift. Of that, we will have more to say momentarily!

It would have been a very easy thing for God to have furnished all the materials Himself, which He could have readily done. Instead, He allowed the Children of Israel to have a part in this great work that would be carried out. It is the same way presently.

The Lord needs nothing! He is dependent on no one or no thing. He is self-sufficient in all things. As well, He is omnipotent (all-powerful), omniscient (all-knowing), and omnipresent (everywhere). So, He certainly needs no help from us, or anything else for that matter.

But yet, He allows us to have a part in His great work, just as He allowed the Children of Israel to have a part in what was to be done, by the giving of their means.

Incidentally, the Children of Israel, although fresh out of Egypt, were flush with gold and silver, as well as precious stones, all given to them by the Egyptians when they left (Ex. 3:21-22).

He has done all of this in a very remarkable way. He wants us to freely give to Him of the labor of our hands, and then He will freely bless us for our giving. In fact, He said to Israel at a later time, and it can be no less to us presently, and even greater: *"Prove Me now herewith, says the LORD of Hosts, if I will not open you the windows of Heaven, and pour you out a blessing, that there shall not be room enough to receive it"* (Mal. 3:10).

THE TYPE OF OFFERING

"And this is the offering which you shall take of them; gold, and silver, and copper,

"And blue, and purple, and scarlet, and fine linen, and goats' hair,

"And rams' skins dyed red, and badgers' skins, and shittim wood,

"Oil for the light, spices for anointing oil, and for sweet incense,

"Onyx stones, and stones to be set in the ephod and in the breastplate" (Ex. 25:3-7).

To understand how the Israelites could supply all that was wanted and needed, we must remember, as we have stated, that just before their departure, they had received large presents of gold and silver, plus many other things, from the Egyptians (Ex. 12:35).

So, in fact, they had an abundance of all that was needed. We need to briefly address that:

As is obvious in Verse 1, the Lord had supplied all of these riches to the Children of Israel, who had been slaves up until a few days before. So, everything they had was given to them by the Lord; therefore, what He was asking of them was that which He had so freely given to them in the first place. It is no different presently!

Whenever the Lord blesses us, and He will definitely do so if we will walk in obedience to His Word, He, even as here, expects us to then help finance His work. However, sadly and regrettably, all too often this isn't done, or else, it isn't done to the degree it ought to be done.

Wealth had been given unto the Children of Israel for several reasons; however, the main reason was that they would be able to finance the building of the Tabernacle and its furnishings, much of which was made out of gold. In fact, everything that went into the Tabernacle was of the finest of materials. Considering the amount of gold used, coupled with everything else, and especially considering the manner in which some items were made, the Tabernacle could easily have cost more than $100 million.

THE SANCTUARY

"And let them make Me a sanctuary; that I may dwell among them" (Ex. 25:8).

As far as is known, the Ark of Noah, the Tabernacle of Moses, and the Temple of Solomon, with the plans actually given to David, are the only buildings ever erected from plans furnished by direct revelation from God (Gen. 6:14-16; I Chron. 28:11-12, 19).

Since the fall of man in the Garden of Eden, the Lord has been working steadily to bring man back to Himself. He longs to dwell with us.

In the Tabernacle and Temple, He dwelt between the Mercy Seat and the Cherubim, which were located in the

Holy of Holies of both the Tabernacle and the Temple. Before the Cross, even as Paul graphically explained in the book of Hebrews, this was as close as God could dwell with man. The reason was the insufficiency of animal blood. Paul also said, *"For it is not possible that the blood of bulls and goats should take away sins"* (Heb. 10:4). In other words, while animal blood served as a stopgap measure until the Cross would come, within itself, it was woefully insufficient to take away sins. Only Christ could do that, which He did by giving Himself on the Cross of Calvary (Jn. 1:29).

However, since the Cross, as should be obvious, the Cross is the centrality of the Gospel. The Holy Spirit can now dwell permanently in the hearts and lives of all believers (Jn. 14:17). The reason is simple: the blood of Jesus Christ atoned for all sin, thereby, taking sin away (Eph. 2:13-18). Paul said, *"Do you not know that you are the temple of God, and that the Spirit of God dwells in you?"* (I Cor. 3:16).

SYMBOLIC OF CHRIST
(Exodus 25:3-8)

Everything that Verses 3 through 8 mention portrays Christ in some manner, whether His atoning work, mediatorial work, or intercessory work.

Verse 3 speaks of *"gold, silver, and brass"* (copper). Gold was symbolic of His deity, silver of the redemption that He would afford for us by His death on the Cross of Calvary, and the copper spoke of the judgment He would suffer on our behalf.

Verse 4 speaks of *"blue,"* which speaks of the fact that He came from Heaven, *"purple"* represents His kingship, and *"scarlet"* represents the blood that He would shed for the salvation of humanity. The *"fine linen"* stands for His righteous-

ness. The *"goats' hair"* came from the Asian goats, which had long, beautiful hair, almost as fine as silk, and valued as much as wool from the sheep. It represented His prophetic office.

In Verse 5, the *"rams' skins"* represented His becoming a sacrificial offering, but yet, as a king. They were dyed red, representing His shed blood. The *"badgers' skins"* were the last covering on the Tabernacle. Looking from the outside, that is what the world saw. It was not very attractive. Likewise, Christ's life as a peasant was not very attractive. Also, as the unbeliever looks at Christianity, there is nothing outwardly that looks attractive, but as the Tabernacle, if one comes inside, the beauty then is overwhelming. The badger skins represented Christ as our Great High Priest.

THE NATURE OF GOD

The *"shittim wood"* came from the acacia tree, which produced a beautiful and durable wood, sometimes called indestructible wood; in other words, it would not rot. It was representative of His perfect, sinless, spotless body.

Verse 6 speaks of *"oil for the light."* This was representative of the Holy Spirit, who rested on Christ above and beyond measure. The *"spices for sweet incense"* spoke of His prayerful and constant intercession on behalf of every child of God.

The *"precious stones"* of Verse 7 that would ultimately go in the ephod and the breastplate were all symbolic of God's grace and glory toward the Children of Israel. This grace and glory can now be made more abundant and more evident to the believer all because of Calvary.

Every part of the Tabernacle was typical of the nature of God: the coming redemption, the sinfulness of man, the means of pardon through grace, and the full reconciliation of man to God. God has always wanted to *"dwell"* with man. Thankfully, a million times over I might say, He dwells within my heart as He does within the hearts and lives of untold millions.

THE PATTERN

"According to all that I show you, after the pattern of the Tabernacle, and the pattern of all the instruments thereof, even so shall you make it" (Ex. 25:9).

The *"pattern"* was all of God and none at all of man. This means that everything about the Tabernacle, down to the finest detail, was designed by God and God alone!

This is symbolic of salvation. It is all of God and none of man, and anything that man attempts to introduce into salvation, other than that which God has already designed, only tends to corrupt the perfection of the plan of God, which means that such salvation is void. God will never accept any of man's patterns; He will only accept His own *"pattern,"* who is Jesus Christ, and more particularly, *Jesus Christ and Him crucified* (I Cor. 1:23).

We Christians are very quick to speak of God blessing us, and well we should; however, in truth, God does not really bless us per se, but actually Christ within us. Everything is in Christ, of Christ, by Christ, with Christ, through Christ, and, in fact, is Christ alone! It is only of Christ and never of man that God has said, *"This is My beloved Son, in whom I am well pleased"* (Mat. 3:17; 17:5; Mk. 1:11; Lk. 3:22).

FAITH

The closest the Scripture comes to saying that God is pleased with man is found in the realm of faith. It is said: *"By faith Enoch was translated that he should not see death; and was not found, because God had translated him: for before his translation he had this testimony, that he pleased God.*

"But without faith it is impossible to please Him: for he who comes to God must believe that He is, and that He is a rewarder of them who diligently seek Him" (Heb. 11:5-6).

However, the actual meaning of what is stated here pertains to faith in Christ and what Christ would do at the Cross in order to redeem lost humanity. Such faith pleases God, and such faith alone pleases God.

So, we can see that it is all in Christ and without Christ, it is impossible to please the Lord, but with Christ, and more particularly, faith in Him and what He has done for us at the Cross, we can please God.

THE BIGGEST SIN

The greatest sin of all is man tampering with the pattern (Rom. 1:18; Heb. 6:4-6; 10:26-29).

When it came to the Tabernacle, the Lord gave to Moses the pattern of all that was to be done, and Moses was not to deviate from that pattern one iota (Ex. 25:40). As stated, this is man's great problem. He tampers with the pattern.

The pattern now is the Cross (I Cor. 1:17-18, 23; 2:2; Rom. 6:1-14; 8:1-11; Gal. 6:14; Col. 2:10-15).

Let me say it again because it is so very, very important. God has given us a pattern for life and living, and that pattern is the Cross of Christ. The believer must understand that every single thing we receive from God comes by the way of Jesus Christ and through the Holy Spirit, all made possible by the Cross. Without the Cross, there is no salvation, no baptism with the Holy Spirit, no divine healing, no fruit of the Spirit, no gifts of the Spirit, no communion with God, and no blessings. In other words, without the Cross, there is nothing! The Cross of Christ is the means and the only means by which everything is made available to us. That is the pattern, and God doesn't have another because no other is needed.

THE WORKMEN

"And the Lord spoke unto Moses, saying,
"See, I have called by name Bezaleel the son of Uri, the son of Hur, of the Tribe of Judah" (Ex. 31:1-2).

These are men called by the Lord for the purpose of building the Tabernacle and, as well, the sacred vessels.

As is obvious, the Lord had a particular person for this work, exactly as He has a particular person for every work of the Kingdom. The work of God is definitely not a volunteer program. Irrespective as to what it is, the Lord has a work for every single believer, always and without exception; it is a *"calling!"* The problem is, we have so many who attempt to do that which the Lord has never called them to do. The result is always confusion, hurt, and an increase of problems.

It seems that Bezaleel was the grandson of Hur, who it is believed was the brother-in-law of Moses, having married his sister Miriam.

As should be obvious by now, the choice of these principle workmen was that of God and not Moses. The pattern for the Tabernacle and all of its accessories was given to Moses, but the building of the apparatus was to be done by another, one chosen by the Lord.

Bezaleel was of the tribe of Judah, which means *"praise."* It was the kingly tribe, from which Christ would come.

In a sense, Moses was a type of Christ, with Bezaleel being a type of the Holy Spirit. Christ was the pattern, and it was the business of the Holy Spirit to make of Him what was intended, i.e., *"the Saviour."*

THE SPIRIT OF GOD

"And I have filled him with the Spirit of God, in wisdom, and in understanding, and in knowledge, and in all manner of workmanship" (Ex. 31:3).

Bezaleel, within himself, could not have carried forth this work. He had to have the Spirit of God in order to accomplish the task. It is the same now with every single believer, who is to satisfy the call of God on his or her life.

Before the Cross, all true believers were in the Covenant; however, due to the fact that the Holy Spirit was limited as to His involvement, all didn't have a specific call. Since the Cross, due to the fact that the Holy Spirit lives within the hearts and lives of all believers, every single believer has a call of some kind from the Lord. That call is definitely not of the fivefold ministry in every case (Eph. 4:11), but it does pertain to a function of some nature.

THE EMPOWERMENT OF THE HOLY SPIRIT

However, to carry out that function, whether it's one of the fivefold callings or otherwise, the believer must have the empowerment of the Holy Spirit. Many take the Holy Spirit for granted, thinking that because He is present, He will just automatically do things. He won't!

The infilling of the Spirit provides potential, but potential only. For us to have His leading, guidance, power, and anointing, we must earnestly seek the face of the Lord, making ourselves available for that which He desires to do. Unfortunately, there isn't a whole lot of consecration among most Christians; consequently, there isn't a lot of leading of the Spirit, but one thing is certain: if we are to carry out the work of God, we must, without fail, have the operation of the Holy Spirit within our lives. He alone can give the wisdom, the understanding, and the knowledge that we need to carry out the task, whatever that task might be.

HOW THE HOLY SPIRIT WORKS

The Holy Spirit works entirely within the framework of the finished work of Christ, and, of course, we are speaking of the Cross. This is what gives Him the legal means to do all that He does for us and with us.

Before the Cross, due to the fact that the blood of bulls and goats could not take away sins (Heb. 10:4), this meant the sin debt remained, despite the consecration of the believer. All during that time, a time frame of some 4,000 years, while the Holy Spirit could be with believers, those who had faith and trust in Christ, so to speak, He could not dwell within them as He now does.

While the Holy Spirit could come into the hearts and lives of some certain people, such as prophets, to help them carry out a specific task, when that was completed, He left.

With the Cross of Christ, this means that all sin was atoned, past, present, and future, at least for all who will believe (Jn. 3:16). This means that all sin was taken away (Jn. 1:29). So, at conversion, the Holy Spirit comes into the believer's heart and life, there to abide forever (Jn. 14:16). However, still, His work within our lives is only potential. It means the potential is there, that is, if we yield to Him.

The Holy Spirit requires one thing of us, which is very, very important. Due to the fact that it is the Cross which has given Him the legal means to do all that He now does, He requires that our faith always and without fail be exclusively in Christ and the Cross, understanding that the Cross has made everything possible (Rom. 6:1-14; 8:1-11; I Cor. 1:17-18, 23; 2:2; Col. 2:10-15).

With our faith planted firmly in the Cross of Christ, the Holy Spirit will then use His almighty power on our behalf.

The believer must understand that as a child of God, we are facing the concentrated powers of darkness. I speak of demon spirits, fallen angels, and even Satan himself (Eph. 6:11-12). If we try to overcome these powerful beings by our own personal strength, we will fail every time, no matter how sincere we might be. It is the Holy Spirit who alone can give us what we need and do for us what we need to have done. Other than that, the believer is going to be ruled by the sin nature, which makes life miserable to say the least.

IN ALL MANNER OF WORKMANSHIP

"To devise cunning works, to work in gold, and in silver, and in brass,

"And in cutting of stones, to set them, and in carving of timber, to work in all manner of workmanship" (Ex. 31:4-5).

In this, we are made to see that the Holy Spirit can help us in whatever task is assigned to us. Of course, we must know that the Holy Spirit is God. This means that He is all-powerful, all-knowing, and everywhere.

In fact, every single thing done on this earth by the Godhead, with the exception of Christ, has been done, carried out, and empowered by the Holy Spirit. And yet, the Holy Spirit oversaw every aspect of our Lord's conception, birth, upbringing, ministry, miracles, etc. In fact, the Holy Spirit told Christ when He could die while on the Cross (Heb. 9:14). Actually, Jesus was placed on the Cross at 9 a.m., the time of the morning sacrifice, and He died at 3 p.m., the time of the evening sacrifice, thereby, fulfilling the Scripture in every capacity. The Holy Spirit superintended all of this, plus the resurrection of Christ and the ascension, in fact, everything pertaining to Christ.

In our text, the Holy Spirit is going to give these men special talent to make after the pattern which the Lord had given to Moses.

WISE HEARTED

"And I, behold, I have given with him Aholiab, the son of Ahisamach, of the tribe of Dan: And in the hearts of all who are wise hearted I have put wisdom, that they may make all that I have commanded you" (Ex. 31:6).

If it is to be noticed, the Lord said here, *"wise hearted,"* instead of, *"wise headed."* This means that the Holy Spirit functioned in the hearts of these individuals, helping them to do all that they were called to do.

Aholiab was *"of the tribe of Dan."* Judah was the first tribe, while Dan brought up the rear; thus, the entirety of Israel was represented here.

There is no doubt that there were other workmen included, but it was Bezaleel who was in charge, with Aholiab assigned to help him. As well, the Lord promised here that all who helped them, however many there were, they would be helped as well!

RESPONSIBLE FOR THE CONSTRUCTION

"The Tabernacle of the congregation, and the Ark of the Testimony, and the Mercy Seat that is thereupon, and all the furniture of the Tabernacle" (Ex. 31:7).

The Tabernacle is mentioned first and then the Ark of the Covenant, along with the Mercy Seat. All of it, in one way or the other, represented Christ in His atoning, mediatorial, and intercessory work. Consequently, Moses was under great restraint that he order Bezaleel, along with Aholiab, to minutely follow the pattern that was given. These men, who were given the Holy Spirit to help them carry out this formidable task, must make certain that the items were constructed correctly, and above all, that the pattern was followed to the proverbial T.

Whereas these two men, along with all of their helpers, were responsible for this construction, in a sense, every single believer presently falls into the same category. As previously stated, we as believers have the Holy Spirit, and as such, He resides within our hearts and lives in order to carry out a specific purpose, and that purpose is *"Christlikeness."* Just exactly as to how this is to be done, only He knows as He carries out the will of God (Rom. 8:26-29).

"Far away the noise of strife upon my ear is falling,
"Then I know the sins of earth be set on every hand;
"Doubt and fear and things of earth in vain to me
    are calling,
"None of these shall move me from Beulah Land."

"Far below the storm of doubt upon the world is beating,
"Sons of men in battle long the enemy withstand;
"Safe am I within the castle of God's Word retreating,
"Nothing then can reach me 'tis Beulah Land."

"Let the stormy breezes blow, their cry cannot alarm me,
"I am safely sheltered here, protected by God's hand;
"Here the sun is always shining, here there's naught
    can harm me,
"I am safe forever in Beulah Land."

"Viewing here the works of God, I sink in contemplation,

"Hearing now His blessed voice, I see the way He planned;

"Dwelling in the Spirit, here I learn of full salvation,

"Gladly will I tarry in Beulah Land."

2

The Curtains

CHAPTER TWO

The Curtains

WE WILL FIND as we go along that every item in the Tabernacle, every work, every ritual, and every ceremony, as well as the physical part of the Tabernacle itself, all held the meaning of Christ. As such, I think there is no description given in the Word of God that can help us understand Christ as does the Tabernacle.

THE VALUE OF THE STUDY OF THE TABERNACLE

One cannot make a serious study of the Tabernacle without coming away with a full understanding of who Christ is and what Christ has done for us. It pictures His work gloriously and completely.

But yet, far too many Christians spend their time studying foolishness, which has no bearing on anything. The pyramids of Egypt are studied minutely. Other places and points of historical interest are held up as great intellectual wonders, with this of which we speak, which is the only reality there is, receiving little study at all.

Of course, it is understandable as to the action and attitude of the world as it regards the things of God, but not as understandable as it regards the church. I would daresay that at this present time, there aren't enough preachers seriously studying the Tabernacle to even count. The church has been so shot through with humanistic psychology that the work of Christ, as it regards redemption, which is the only answer, is all but totally ignored. Oh yes, Jesus is held up as the great example, and even the provider of money, but with most, that's about as far as it goes. In many charismatic circles, it is even stated that the Old Testament has no value for present-day study. The absurdity of such thinking beggars description! In fact, if one doesn't understand the Old Testament, then it's impossible for one to understand the New Testament.

PERSONAL TESTIMONIES

George Needham says: *"The typical portions of Scripture are supremely important and as a study vastly interesting. Types are shadows. Shadows imply substance. A type has its lessons. It was the design of Jehovah to express His great thought of redemption to His people Israel in a typical or symbolic manner.*

"By laws, ceremonies, institutions, persons, and incidents, He sought to keep alive in Israel's hearts the hope of a coming Redeemer. Christ is therefore the key to Moses' Gospel. This then is our advantage, that we can minutely compare type and antitype, and learn thereby the lessons of grace which bring salvation."

Pink said: *"By means of the Tabernacle, Jehovah revealed His character and made known His purpose of redemption. There, devouring holiness and righteous indignation against sin, declared the fact that God was 'just' even while He justified.*

"The Tabernacle was the place of sacrifice; its most vivid spectacle was the flowing and sprinkling of blood, pointing forward to the sufferings and death of Christ.

"It was also the place of cleansing; there was the blood for atonement, and also the water for washing away the stains of defilement. So Christ 'loved the church and gave Himself for it, that He might sanctify and cleanse it, with the washing of water by the Word; that He might present it to Himself a glorious church, not having spot or wrinkle, or any such thing, but that it should be holy and without blemish'" (Eph. 5:25-27).

THE GREATEST LESSON

The Tabernacle presents the way in which the sinner might approach God, and in that is its most outstanding lesson. We are reminded here that sin has separated man from God and, as well, that there is only one way that God can be approached. That is by the blood of the slain lamb, which typified the Cross of Christ. The blood would be taken into the Holy of Holies once a year by the high priest, who, as well, typified Christ.

Paul's writings so much proclaimed the fact of Christ and His work. For instance, he said *"I determined not to know anything among you save Jesus Christ* (His person) *and Him crucified* (His work)" (I Cor. 2:2). And then in John's visions, he said, *"I beheld ... and in the midst of the Elders, stood a Lamb* (His person) *as it had been slain* (His work)" (Rev. 5:6).

Thus it was in this order of the Tabernacle furniture: first, the Ark, which tells of Christ's person; then the Mercy Seat, which we will study momentarily, which points to His work; and, with the Brazen Altar coming later, which will tell us how He performed His work, which speaks of the Cross. It must be remembered that the high priest could not approach the Ark of the Covenant until he first went by the Brazen Altar and secured the blood of the sacrifice, which, of course, speaks of the Cross. In other words, it is the Cross alone which opens the door to the very throne room of God.

THE CROSS

The Cross is the meeting place between God and man. It is the point where grace and righteousness meet and perfectly harmonize.

TEN CURTAINS

"Moreover you shall make the Tabernacle with ten curtains of fine twined linen, and blue, and purple, and scarlet: With Cherubims of cunning work shall you make them.

"The length of one curtain shall be eight and twenty cubits, and the width of one curtain four cubits: and every one of the curtains shall have one measure.

"The five curtains shall be coupled together one to another; and other five curtains shall be coupled one to another" (Ex. 26:1-3).

While the Scripture is not perfectly clear on the subject, it seems that these *"ten curtains"* had to do with the inner covering of the Tabernacle. They were elaborately embroidered and joined together.

It would seem that the next description after the Lampstand would be the walls of the Tabernacle, but the Lord's ways are not our ways. Everything He does is perfect, and He has a reason for doing it in the manner in which it is done, whatever it might be.

It is the business and obligation of believers to allow the Holy Spirit to work in our lives to such an extent that we begin to see things as the Lord sees them and, in effect, to think like Him, at least as far as is possible to do so.

Each of these curtains was 42 feet long and six feet wide. They were coupled together in fives, thus giving a total length of 42 feet and width of 60 feet. This would not only reach across the Tabernacle, which was 15 feet wide, but would overlap its sides, which they were intended to do. The 60 feet had to do with the length of the Tabernacle, which was 45 feet long, and then with the curtains draped over the back, it would take up the full 60 feet.

The two sets of five white curtains were linked together by 50 loops of blue in each, which were fastened with 50 taches or clasps of gold, thus, firmly uniting the whole together in one solid piece.

FINE TWINED LINEN

This linen was not merely linen, but rather *"fine linen,"* linen of peculiar excellency.

This linen was perfectly white and typified the perfect righteousness of Christ, which, as well, typifies the righteousness of the saints, that is, if their faith is totally in Christ and what He has done for us at the Cross (Rev. 19:8).

Cherubim were to be woven into the material, using the colors of *"blue, and purple, and scarlet."* The *"blue"* represented the fact that all salvation comes from Heaven and not at all from this earth, meaning that Christ was all of Heaven.

"Purple" speaks of royalty, meaning that Jesus Christ was a king, as well, in effect, *"the King."*

The *"scarlet"* speaks of blood and, thereby, the sufferings of Christ. Of course, the Cherubim denote His holiness.

So, in these curtains, we have righteousness, holiness, the heavenly, the kingly, and, as well, the Cross.

THE CHERUBIM AND THE COLORS

BEAUTIFUL

As the Golden Lampstand illuminated the holy place, the white would have been brilliant, with the colors standing out in bold relief, all typifying Christ and portraying the beauty that would not be seen from the outside. In fact, there was nothing beautiful about the Tabernacle on the outside. All beauty was reserved for the interior.

So the world looks at Christ, *"And there is no beauty that they should desire Him,"* at least outwardly, but the Tabernacle tells us differently. It tells us that He is beautiful beyond compare, all typified by the white linen and the beautiful colors of the Cherubim. However, one has to come inside the Tabernacle, i.e., *"into Christ,"* which can only be done in the born-again experience, before one can fully know what and who Christ actually is.

Without this revelation, Christ is just another figure in history, and a peasant at that! However, to those who have accepted Him as Lord and Saviour, we know Him to be of such beautiful composure as to defy all description.

When He came the first time, He came as the outward appearance of the Tabernacle. There was little attraction there. However, when He comes the second time, which Revelation, Chapter 19, describes, He will come as *"King of kings and Lord of lords,"* which refers to a power, glory, and beauty beyond compare.

THE LENGTH AND WIDTH OF THE CURTAINS

The length of one curtain was 28 cubits, and its width was four cubits.

"*Seven,*" God's perfect number, goes four times into the length, with the curtains, as well, being four cubits wide. This speaks of the perfection of "*seven*" and the completeness of "*four.*"

Edward Dennett said concerning this: "*The curtains of the Tabernacle, consequently, speak of the complete unfolding perfections of Christ as man when passing through this scene.*"

THE REASON

I personally believe that the reason the Lord gave the dimensions of the curtains first before He went to the walls is because the curtains form the ceiling of the Tabernacle. This suggests that the curtains set before us the one who humbled Himself and became obedient unto death, but who is now called and glorified on high.

In John's visions, we have an idea of what all of this means:

- John saw Christ in His glory (Rev. 1:12-17).
- He saw Him as "*a Lamb as it had been slain ...*" (Rev. 5:6).

This tells us that the glory and beauty of Christ cannot be properly seen except through His Cross. As beautiful as it is, the white linen, which spoke of His righteousness, typifies His perfection in every capacity, but especially as it regards the sacrifice. The "*blue*" tells us that there was none on earth worthy to offer himself in sacrifice, so one would have to come from Heaven, who is the Lord Jesus Christ. The "*purple*" speaks of His kingship, but yet, He could not have been

THE LOOPS AND COUPLINGS

King unless He had gone to the Cross. The *"scarlet"* speaks of the price that He paid, leading us directly to the Cross.

So, even though the ceiling was beautiful beyond compare, which pictures Christ as it could only picture Christ, it all portrays His atoning work on the Cross, which the Cherubim address by constantly saying, *"Holy, Holy, Holy."*

THE LOOPS

"And you shall make loops of blue upon the edge of the one curtain from the selvedge in the coupling; and likewise shall you make in the uttermost edge of another curtain, in the coupling of the second.

"Fifty loops shall you make in the one curtain, and fifty loops shall you make in the edge of the curtain that is in the coupling of the second; that the loops may take hold one of another.

"And you shall make fifty taches of gold, and couple the curtains together with the taches: And it shall be one Tabernacle" (Ex. 26:4-6).

As would be obvious, the loops were appointed for the joining of the curtains together.

The ten curtains arranged in two sets of five each point out something to us.

The meaning of the number *"ten"* is that of human responsibility.

As an example, we see that there were *"ten plagues upon Egypt,"* with Pharaoh continuing to rebel, which demonstrated the failure of his responsibility. He and his hosts were destroyed at the Red Sea.

In these last days, the Scripture tells us that Gentile domination will consist of "ten kingdoms," and then will be fully manifested in the breakdown of its responsibility.

God gave *"Ten Commandments"* to the human race. The first five pertain to man's responsibility to God, with the second five pertaining to our responsibility to our fellowman.

CHRIST

Consequently, the ten curtains speak of Christ as the representative of His people, meeting the whole of our obligations both Godward and manward. He loved God with all of His heart and His neighbor as Himself. He was the only one by whom these responsibilities were fully and perfectly met.

The loops were blue, the color of Heaven, again signifying that everything we have from the Lord came entirely from Heaven and none at all from earth, even though its consummation was on earth, and I speak of the Cross.

The word *"taches"* means *"couplings."* They were made of gold, and they united the curtains together as they were passed through the loops of blue.

All of this may seem insignificant; however, without these loops and couplings, the beautiful curtains would have hung apart one from another, and thus, the one main feature of their manifestation would have been lost.

These couplings fastened the whole of the 10 curtains together so that they were *"one Tabernacle."* Thus, they pointed to the blessed unity and uniformity of the character and life of Christ.

The 50 loops were expressed by the number *"five"* and its multiples. As we shall see, there were 50 boards, 15 bars, and 100 sockets. There were 50 loops, 50 taches of gold, and 50 taches of copper. As we have stated, five is the number of grace, which denotes this Tabernacle, and is the attribute of Christ (Jn. 1:17).

GOATS' HAIR

"And you shall make curtains of goats' hair to be a covering upon the Tabernacle: eleven curtains shall you make" (Ex. 26:7).

The *"goats' hair"* covering was totally hidden from view. It signified Christ's prophetic office. Even though He definitely was a prophet and, in fact, the greatest prophet of all, as would be obvious, He was not recognized or seen as such! Israel rejected Him and would not own Him at all. When He predicted that He would be killed in Jerusalem and then would rise from the dead on the third day, His own disciples rebuked Him (Mat. 16:21-23).

GOATS' HAIR COVERING

It was at this time that Jesus said: *"If any man will come after Me, let him deny himself, and take up his cross, and follow Me"* (Mat. 16:24).

In effect, He was telling His disciples not only that He would be killed, but also that the Cross would be used to bring about this terrible crime.

However, we must quickly say that while murder was in the heart of the Jews, they, in effect, did not take His life from Him; He purposely laid it down (Jn. 10:17-18).

So, as the goats' hair covering was hidden from view, likewise, the prophetic office of Christ was also hidden from view as well!

Whereas 10 curtains had been joined together to make the ceiling of fine twined linen, 11 curtains were to be used as it regarded the goats' hair covering.

Why 11 curtains? The next two verses provide some small clue.

DOUBLE

"The length of one curtain shall be thirty cubits, and the breadth of one curtain four cubits: and the eleven curtains shall be all of one measure.

"And you shall couple five curtains by themselves, and six curtains by themselves, and shall double the sixth curtain in the forefront of the Tabernacle" (Ex. 26:8-9).

The idea of the eleventh curtain seems to be twofold.

These coverings or curtains seem to have been laid crosswise over the Tabernacle, with the ends hanging down on both sides. In other words, there was no hip roof on the Tabernacle, with the top being flat, which the top was actually the coverings.

The adding of the eleventh curtain created enough extra width that it could be doubled at the forefront, which referred to it being pulled under the linen covering. This would provide greater protection from the elements.

The width of the goats' hair curtains was the same as the linen curtains, but the goats' hair curtains were two cubits longer.

The Tabernacle itself was 30 cubits long (45 feet), 10 cubits wide (15 feet), and 10 cubits high (15 feet).

Due to being 28 cubits, the linen curtain would not come down all the way to the ground on either side of the Tabernacle. However, the goats' hair covering being 30 cubits, which is 45 feet, it would cover the Tabernacle and the sides completely, actually reaching to the ground on either side, thereby, giving it proper protection.

The prophetic ministry of Christ was perfect in every respect and, in fact, the only perfect prophetic ministry that has ever existed. The earthly ministry of Christ, as it refers to prophecy, dealt with every single aspect of the human condition, which was to come, and, as well, the complexities of the state of Israel (Mat., Chpt. 24). So, as the goats' hair covering was total, likewise, so was the prophetic ministry of Christ!

THE LOOPS AND THE TACHES

"And you shall make fifty loops to the edge of the one curtain that is outmost in the coupling, and fifty loops in the edge of the curtain which couples the second.

"And you shall make fifty taches of brass, and put the taches into the loops, and couple the tent together, that it may be one.

"And the remnant that remains of the curtain of the tent, the half curtain that remains, shall hang over the backside of the Tabernacle.

"And a cubit on the one side, and a cubit on the other side of that which remains in the length of the curtains of the tent, it shall hang over the sides of the Tabernacle on this side and on that side, to cover it" (Ex. 26:10-13).

The *"fifty loops"* joined the portions together, which means that the two portions of the goats' hair covering were to be united in exactly the same way as those of the inner awning of linen.

In the linen covering, the *"taches"* were of gold, while the taches here are of copper.

While copper can speak of judgment, it also can speak of humanity, and that is the meaning I believe is given here. Deity does not function in the realm of prophecy. Deity is omniscient, meaning that it knows everything — past, present, and future. The prophetic office could only be held by a man or a woman, in this case, the Lord Jesus Christ, which spoke of His humanity, i.e., *"the Incarnation."*

RAMS' SKINS AND BADGERS' SKINS

"And you shall make a covering for the tent of rams' skins dyed red, and a covering above of badgers' skins" (Ex. 26:14).

If it is to be noticed, while dimensions were given as it regarded the linen and the goats' hair coverings, no dimensions are given regarding the rams' and badgers' skin coverings. More than likely, they were the same size as the goats' hair coverings. But yet, the dimensions were left off for a purpose and reason.

RAMS' SKINS AND BADGERS' SKINS

Could this not intimate that what these coverings foreshadowed was beyond our power to measure? There was a depth and a height in our Saviour's devotion to God and in His humiliation before men that is utterly impossible for us to gauge.

The rams' skins dyed red typified Christ as king. Due to the fact that they were dyed red, this tells us that it was a king who died on the Cross for lost humanity. And yet, Israel laughed at His kingship. However, had they checked the genealogies in the Temple, they would have known that had the Davidic dynasty continued, Joseph would have been king, and Jesus, as the eldest son, would have followed suit. In fact, the Holy Spirit referred to Him as the *"Son of David"* (Mat. 1:1).

JESUS

Jesus was not popular! The multitude might have followed Him for a short time because, in their judgment, His ministry stood connected with *"the loaves and fishes,"* which met their needs. However, another crowd would shortly say, *"Away with Him!"*

None of this moved Him simply because He was on this earth to carry out the will of the Father. He was the only perfect servant who ever stood in God's vineyard. He had one object, which He pursued with an undeviating course from the manger to the Cross, and that was to glorify the Father and to finish His work, which He did!

BADGERS' SKINS

The badgers' skins were, no doubt, the same size as the rams' skins and were the last covering to go over the Tabernacle. So, in effect, there were four coverings which made up the top of the Tabernacle:

1. The fine twined linen.
2. The goats' hair.
3. The rams' skin.
4. The badgers' skin.

If in fact the goats' hair covering typified the prophetic office of Christ, and the rams' skins typified that of the office of king, then the badgers' skins had to denote the office of high priest. These were the three roles filled by Christ in His atoning work.

Admittedly, and considering that Christ came from the tribe of Judah and not from the priestly tribe of Levi, He did not look like a high priest or, in reality, a priest of any kind. Neither did He fit the mold of a king or a prophet. While He was all of this, His demeanor was different in every aspect. In fact, His office as king, even though as real then as it will be in the future, still will not come to fruition until the coming Kingdom Age. As well, His role as high priest did not begin until after His ascension, with the Scripture saying: *"But this man* (Jesus), *because He continues ever, has an unchangeable priesthood* (He will always be high priest).

"Wherefore He is able also to save them to the uttermost who come unto God by Him, seeing He ever lives to make intercession for them.

"For such an high priest became us, who is holy, harmless, undefiled, separate from sinners, and made higher than the heavens;

"Who needs not daily, as those high priests (those of Israel) *to offer up sacrifice, first for his own sins, and then*

for the people's: for this He did once, when He offered up Himself" (Heb. 7:25-27).

NO BEAUTY

The last covering, which was of badgers' skins, was appropriate for three reasons.

Of all the coverings over the Tabernacle, this particular covering was the least of all as it regarded ostentatiousness and beauty. In fact, the goats' hair covering was beautiful, which looked almost like silk. As well, the rams' skin coverings had a regal beauty, especially considering that they were dyed red, but the badgers' skins pointed to no beauty whatsoever. This means that the great offices of prophet, king, and high priest, while definitely present, were not obvious at all.

The badgers' skin coverings point to the fact, *"There is no beauty that we should desire Him"* (Isa. 53:2). So, when the passerby looked at the Tabernacle, there would have been nothing there that had attraction. If anything at all, the badgers' skins definitely had no attraction.

WHAT DOES THIS TELL US?

While outwardly the Tabernacle had no attraction, to be sure, the interior was beautiful beyond compare. Such is Bible Christianity!

When the unredeemed look at Christianity from the outside, for that's the only way it can be observed from that point, they see absolutely nothing that sparks their interest. However, once they come to Christ, the beauty and the glory of this Christian experience then become very obvious, and the only regret they have is that they didn't come to Christ sooner!

Secondly, the badgers' skins tell us that this Christian experience, even though it is wonderful and glorious, in fact, the greatest thing on earth, still, it is nothing by comparison to what will be given to us at the coming Resurrection. That's why Paul said: *"But ourselves also, which have the firstfruits of the Spirit, even we ourselves groan within ourselves, waiting for the adoption, to wit, the redemption of our body"* (Rom. 8:23).

Finally, the badgers' skins spoke of humility, as should be obvious. This was the only thing that the Master ever said of Himself: *"For I am meek and lowly in heart"* (Mat. 11:29).

The world looks at the outside of everything because that's all it has, but Christ directs us to the miracle of transformation, typified by the interior of the Tabernacle.

> *"Rock of Ages cleft for me,*
> *"Let me hide myself in Thee;*
> *"Let the waters and the blood,*
> *"From Your riven side which flowed,*
> *"Be of sin the double cure,*
> *"Saved from wrath and make me pure."*

> *"Not the labors of my hands,*
> *"Can fulfill Your law's demands;*
> *"Could my zeal no respite know,*
> *"Could my tears forever flow,*
> *"All for sin could not atone,*
> *"You must save, and You alone."*

"Nothing in my hand I bring,
"Simply to Your Cross I cling;
"Naked, come to You for dress:
"Helpless, look to You for grace;
"Foul, I to the fountain fly;
"Wash me, Saviour, or I die!"

"While I draw this fleeting breath,
"When my eyes shall close in death,
"When I soar to world's unknown,
"See Thee on Your judgment throne,
"Rock of Ages cleft for me,
"Let me hide myself in Thee."

3

The Boards

CHAPTER THREE

The Boards

"AND YOU SHALL *make boards for the Tabernacle of shittim wood standing up.*

"*Ten cubits shall be the length of a board, and a cubit and a half shall be the breadth of one board.*

"*Two tenons shall there be in one board, set in order one against another: thus shall you make for all the boards of the Tabernacle.*

"*And you shall make the boards for the Tabernacle, twenty boards on the south side southward.*

"*And you shall make forty sockets of silver under the twenty boards; two sockets under one board for his two tenons, and two sockets under another board for his two tenons*" (Ex. 26:15-19).

We now come to the framework and foundation of the Tabernacle proper. In fact, it was a simple arrangement. There were 50 boards in all: 20 on the south side, 20 on the north side, six on the west end, with two boards on each corner at the back, making 50 in all.

The boards were 15 feet high and about 27 inches wide. We aren't told how thick they were.

The boards were of indestructible wood which came from the acacia tree. They were overlaid with gold (Ex. 26;29) thereby portraying the manhood of Christ (typified by the wood) and the deity of Christ (typified by the gold).

THE HAND

The Hebrew word for *"tenon"* is *"yad"* and means *"an open hand."* There were two of them under each board, making a total of 100 tenons. The Scripture doesn't say of what type of metal they were made; however, they were probably made of silver.

Each board overlaid with gold, with the tenons under each corner, were set into two sockets of silver.

It is believed that each socket of silver weighed about a talent, which is about 120 pounds. This would have provided a tremendous foundation, which was intended!

SILVER

If there were 50 boards and two sockets of silver for each board, this would have made 100 sockets, which formed the foundation, and upon them rested the whole fabric of the Tabernacle.

Silver was meant to represent redemption, which is evidenced more clearly in Exodus, Chapter 30, as it regards the *"shekel of the sanctuary,"* which was the ransom money for each person. The idea was not that redemption could be purchased by man but, in fact, that it was purchased by the Lord Jesus Christ, who at that time, of course, had not yet come.

All of this tells us that redemption is the basis on which Christ has become the meeting place between the thrice-holy God and His inherently unholy people. It is only through redemption that the perfect humanity and divine glory of Christ could bring us to Himself. John 12:24 tells us that Christ could multiply Himself only by dying, which He did, which *"brought forth much fruit."*

Redemption and the Crucifixion are intertwined, so to speak. Paul, angry at the Galatians for turning away from the truth of the Cross to other things, said: *"O foolish Galatians, who has bewitched you, that you should not obey the truth, before whose eyes Jesus Christ has been evidently set forth, crucified among you?"* (Gal. 3:1).

If you will notice, Paul didn't say, *"Jesus Christ has been evidently set forth, resurrected among you."* I say that because certain ones claim that salvation is in the Resurrection.

THE CROSS OF CHRIST

Of course, the Resurrection is of supreme significance. That should go without stating. However, I remind the reader that Paul says here, and many places elsewhere, that the Cross must be set before us, and not the suffering in the Garden, the Resurrection, as wonderful as that was; the Ascension, or the Exaltation of Christ at the throne of God. While all of these things were absolutely necessary and, of course, are supremely important, it was the crucified Christ which purchased our redemption, and nothing else. That's why the apostle also said:

"But God forbid that I should glory, save in the Cross of our Lord Jesus Christ, by whom the world is crucified unto me, and I unto the world" (Gal. 6:14).

It is my feeling that the so-called Word of Faith doctrine is the doctrine of the last days, set forth by Satan to attempt to pull the church away from the Cross, and it has by and large succeeded. Paul said: **"Now the Spirit (Holy Spirit) speaks expressly (pointedly), that in the latter times** *(the times in which we now live)* **some shall depart from the faith** *(Jesus Christ and Him crucified)* **giving heed to seducing spirits, and doctrines of demons"** (I Tim. 4:1).

"Seducing spirits" are successful simply because they appear as angels of light (II Cor. 11:13-15).

The only salvation for the church is to come back to the Cross. To be sure, the Cross is not one of several ways; it is the only way!

THE PRECIOUS BLOOD OF CHRIST

The *"atonement money"* in Exodus, Chapter 30, does not imply that salvation can be purchased. The Scripture plainly tells us: *"You were not redeemed with corruptible things, as silver and gold ... But with the precious blood of Christ, as of a Lamb without blemish and without spot"* (I Pet. 1:18-19).

The old Law also said: *"For it is the blood that makes an atonement for the soul"* (Lev. 17:11).

So, why did the Holy Spirit use silver as a form of atonement?

It was done for two reasons:

1. It proclaimed the *"preciousness"* of Christ's atonement simply because silver and gold are the most valuable commodities in commerce.

2. While silver and gold couldn't purchase redemption, as stated, most definitely it was purchased, but by the precious blood of Christ. So, the silver here represents redemption, even as, in a sense, the entirety of the Tabernacle represents Christ and redemption. Let it be understood, the Tabernacle did not merely represent Christ, but Christ and the manner in which He would redeem fallen humanity.

COUPLINGS

"And for the second side of the Tabernacle on the north side there shall be 20 boards:

"And there are forty sockets of silver; two sockets under one board, and two sockets under another board.

"And for the sides of the Tabernacle westward you shall make six boards.

"And two boards shall you make for the corners of the Tabernacle in the two sides.

"And they shall be coupled together beneath, and they shall be coupled together above the head of it unto one ring: Thus shall it be for them both; they shall be for the two corners.

"And they shall be eight boards, and their sockets of silver, sixteen sockets; two sockets under one board, and two sockets under another board" (Ex. 26:20-25).

If it is to be noticed, there were no boards on the eastern end of the Tabernacle. In fact, there were five pillars there,

THE COUPLINGS

with the entire front covered by a curtain, which we will look into momentarily. The Tabernacle was to always face the east; therefore, this was the entrance as well.

Also, if it is to be noticed, we have given the *"cubit"* a measurement of 18 inches, which, of course, is a foot and one-half. It is doubtful that it was exactly that, but, more than likely, that's about as close as we can come in today's modern measurements.

As would be obvious, the *"couplings"* held all the boards together. This had to do with the *"tenons"* or *"hands,"* as well as the sockets of silver, at least on the bottom. At the top, one of the *"bars,"* which we will study momentarily, held everything in place.

THE LORD JESUS CHRIST

All of this proclaimed and prefigured the God-Man, the Lord Jesus Christ, who in His voluntary humiliation, would be dependent upon and in subjection to the Father. As the perfect servant, He was upheld and sustained by the hands of God the Father from above with the Spirit below ministering to Him. Of old, the Spirit of Prophecy cried, *"Let Your Hand be upon the Man of Your right hand, upon the Son of Man whom You made strong for Yourself"* (Ps. 80:17). As well, our Lord said: *"My times are in Your hand"* (Ps. 31:15). And then, from the Cross: *"Father, into Your hands I commend My Spirit"* (Lk. 23:46). And now, He is seated on *"the right hand of the Majesty on high"* (Heb. 1:3)!

As we've already stated, the Tabernacle represented Christ not only in its entirety but, more than all, presented Christ in His atoning, mediatorial, and intercessory work. In other words, it represented Him in what He would do in order to redeem fallen humanity. The entire reason for His coming to this earth, thereby, becoming man, was in order to redeem fallen humanity. To be sure, none of this was done for Himself, for Heaven, for angels, etc. It was all done for sinners. This tells us that man's problem is sin, and the solution alone is the Saviour, the Lord Jesus Christ, and what He did for us at Calvary.

So, in essence, all of these boards proclaimed the various aspects of the ministry of Christ in some way, and one could say, I think, the benefits of the Cross. Those benefits are literally inexhaustible!

THE FIVE BARS

"And you shall make bars of shittim wood; five for the boards of the one side of the Tabernacle,

"And five bars for the boards of the other side of the Tabernacle, and five bars for the boards of the side of the Tabernacle, for the two sides westward.

"And the middle bar in the midst of the board shall reach from end to end" (Ex. 26:26-28).

The order of these bars seem to have been as follows:

The *"middle bar"* of the five, which would run horizontal in the middle from end to end, would be approximately 45 feet long. This united and held all the 20 boards together, at least on the south and north sides. It would be the same with the west end, although a much shorter distance of only 15 feet.

The other four bars, two below and two above, are not described as running all the length, but perhaps only extended half the distance, in other words, being in two pieces, although extending the entire length of the Tabernacle.

GRACE

The five bars symbolized the grace of God, with grace made possible to us through Christ by what He did for us at the Cross. In other words, the Cross, of which the Tabernacle is a type, opened up the way for grace to be given in an unlimited way to the believer. God has always had grace, and, in fact, every single thing He has ever given man has come through grace. However, before the Cross, due to the sin debt remaining, grace could not be extended as abundantly as it is now since the Cross.

The five bars could also represent the fivefold callings: apostles, prophets, evangelists, pastors, and teachers (Eph. 4:11).

These are referred to as *"gifts"* (Eph. 4:8), which, of course, speaks of grace.

In other words, as individuals are called by God to be one of these offices, which is supposed to be, *"For the perfecting of the saints, for the work of the ministry, for the edifying of the Body of Christ,"* we must conclude this to be grace (Eph. 4:12).

If these offices function as they should function, they will proclaim Christ in every capacity and, above all, His finished work at the Cross. In fact, that is their very purpose.

RINGS OF GOLD

"And you shall overlay the boards with gold, and make their rings of gold for places for the bars: and you shall overlay the bars with gold" (Ex. 26:29).

The *"rings of gold"* were evidently attached to the boards through which the bars passed. As to how many rings there were to each link, we aren't told. As everything about the Tabernacle pertained to Christ in His atoning and mediatorial work, we know that these rings of gold had a spiritual meaning as well.

RINGS AND BARS OF GOLD

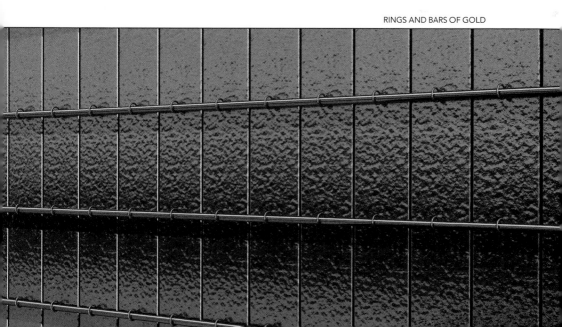

More than likely, they pertained to the work of the Spirit in connecting all the ministries of Christ. Even though our Saviour had different ministries, all ultimately played out to Christ as Saviour. The *"bars,"* which held all of this together, were themselves held in place by rings of gold.

The ultimate work of Christ was salvation for lost humanity. He would accomplish this task by and through the Cross, even though every aspect of His multifaceted ministry contributed to the ultimate goal.

We must allow this to be a lesson to us, as well, that these rings of gold still apply spiritually, hence, Paul saying: *"For Christ sent me not to baptize, but to preach the Gospel: not with wisdom of words, lest the Cross of Christ should be made of none effect"* (I Cor. 1:17).

THE FASHION

"And you shall rear up the Tabernacle according to the fashion thereof which was shewed you in the mount" (Ex. 26:30).

This is basically the same statement as was given in Exodus 25:40. As stated, the repetition is for purpose and is, therefore, brought forth by design.

As in the previous verse, the Holy Spirit is saying that all of the instructions given here to Moses by God were to be held to exactly. In other words, Moses must not add anything to the design or take something from the design. It was all of God and none of man.

As well, Moses was to minutely inspect each thing done by the craftsmen that they not deviate from the pattern at all.

This beautifully symbolizes salvation and, as well, points to the great problem of the church, and mankind in general.

As Cain of old, man is not satisfied with the plan of salvation brought forth by God but feels that he must complement that pattern in some way or ignore it altogether. To be sure, when men attempt to add to or take away, soon there is nothing left that was originally given by God.

This has always been a problem for the church, but I suspect it is more of a problem now than ever before. As a case in point, we will look at humanistic psychology.

Peter said: *"According as His divine power has given unto us all things that pertain unto life and godliness, through the knowledge of Him who has called us to glory and virtue:*

"Whereby are given unto us exceeding great and precious promises, that by these you might be partakers of the divine nature, having escaped the corruption that is in the world through lust" (II Pet. 1:3-4).

In essence, this means that Jesus addressed at the Cross every single problem that besets fallen humanity (Col. 2:14-15). However, several decades ago, the church, losing faith in the Cross because it was not faithfully preached, began to turn to humanistic psychology. Today, that particular direction is almost complete, which means that the entirety of the church has gone in that direction. Of course, there is an exception here and there, but those exceptions are few and far between.

HUMANISTIC PSYCHOLOGY

Using preachers as an example, if the preacher, through lack of knowledge of the Cross, is overcome by the powers of darkness, instead of that preacher being directed to the Cross, he will be directed toward humanistic psychology. And here is the clincher: if he doesn't go that route, the church, for all practical purposes, will write him off, in effect, blackballing him and doing everything within their power to destroy whatever vestige of ministry that might remain.

This erroneous direction is not content to merely proclaim their false way, thereby, deceiving the people, but they are also intent upon destroying anything that opposes that false way.

All of this goes back to the saga of Cain and Abel (Gen. Chpt. 4).

According to the directions of the Lord, both Cain and Abel offered a sacrifice, but Cain departed from the type of sacrifice demanded by God. He produced the fruit of his own hands instead, which God could not accept. If the sacrifice was rejected, which it was, then the one offering the sacrifice was rejected, as well, the standard, which holds to this very hour.

However, Cain wasn't satisfied with his position of holding up a sacrifice of his own making, but rather felt that he had to destroy Abel, who, in fact, had offered the correct sacrifice. Consequently, he murdered his own brother. That spirit continues in the church and, in fact, has been the overriding spirit from then until now.

If men reject the Cross, and I continue to speak of the church, they attempt to destroy those who are preaching the Cross and will use any means at their disposal to carry out their wicked design. As stated, the murderous intent of Cain continues to abide in the hearts of all who oppose the Cross.

AN ERRONEOUS INTERPRETATION

Many Christians have an erroneous interpretation of the Tabernacle, thinking it represents Israel, the House of God, the church as a whole, etc. They conclude, as well, that the boards represent the individual members of the church and the central bar, the divine life that makes them one. However, the statement by the Holy Spirit in Psalms 29:9, that every whit of this structure uttered Christ's praise, thereby, militates against that false interpretation.

"Pass me not, O gentle Saviour,
"Hear my humble cry;
"While on others You are calling,
"Do not pass me by."

"Let me at thy throne of mercy,
"Find a sweet relief;
"Kneeling there in deep contrition,
"Help my unbelief."

"Trusting only in Your merit,
"Would I seek Your face;
"Heal my wounded broken spirit,
"Save me by Your grace."

"You the spring of all my comfort,
"More than life to me;
"Whom have I on earth beside Thee?
"Whom in Heaven but Thee?"

4
The Veil

CHAPTER FOUR

The Veil

"AND YOU SHALL make a veil of blue, and purple, and scarlet, and fine twined linen of cunning work: with Cherubims shall it be made" (Ex. 26:31).

This was the inner Veil that separated the Holy Place, which was the first room from the Holy of Holies, which was the second room.

This *"Veil,"* in effect, announced to all that the way of approach to God was not then made known. However, inasmuch as it was a curtain and not a wall of stone or metal, there was more than a hint given of its temporary nature and that a way of access would ultimately be revealed. To be sure, it was, and that way was made possible by what Jesus did on the Cross.

This speaks of the veil that was in the Temple at the time of Christ, which it is believed was approximately 30 feet high and 30 feet wide (I Ki. 6:20). Concerning the death of Christ on the Cross, the Scripture says: *"Jesus, when He had cried again with a loud voice, yielded up the ghost."*

It then said: *"And, behold, the veil of the Temple was rent in twain from the top to the bottom; and the earth did quake, and the rocks rent"* (Mat. 27:50-51).

It was the death of Christ on the Cross alone that could open up the way to the very presence of God as it regarded sinful man. By the giving of Himself in sacrifice, He atoned for all sin, which then made it possible for man to enter into the very presence of God, which, heretofore, was impossible!

The giving here of the colors is identical to that of Exodus 26:1 concerning the curtains, but with one exception. In connection with the curtains, the *"fine twined linen"* was mentioned first; here it is mentioned last.

THE COLORS

Concerning this Pink says, *"This seems to intimate that our attention now is to be concentrated more on what was prefigured by the blue and purple and scarlet, rather than on what was foreshadowed by the linen itself. The colors told of Heaven, the Cross, and the throne. Probably the colors were used so freely that little of the white linen would be visible."*

The *"blue"* signified that this great plan of redemption was all of Heaven and none of earth. The *"purple"* signified the royalty of Christ as king. The *"scarlet"* signified the price that He would pay by the shedding of His blood on the Cross of Calvary.

The *"fine twined linen"* spoke of the humanity of Christ in His perfection. The whiteness of the pure linen used in the Veil pointed to the sinless purity of *"the Man Christ Jesus,"* both in His inward thoughts and desires and in His outward ways and works.

Jesus was what man ought to be and what God intended! The Veil, therefore, was a fitting type that Christ incarnate was perfect God and perfect man.

The object of a *"veil"* is to hide. *"Come not"* (Lev. 16:2) was the warning that it consistently gave forth. Thus, the Veil foreshadowed the moral glories of the Saviour but, at the same time, showed by the very display of such heavenliness of character how far fallen man was away from God.

The perfect manhood of Christ exhibited the only humanity which can approach unto God, which can live in His presence, and which can dwell in the blazing light of His manifested glory. So, the perfections of the God/Man only serve to emphasize the imperfections of fallen man.

THE CROSS

As should be obvious, the Veil was never meant to give access to God; actually, it was that which prevented it.

This proclaims to us that the perfection of the life of Christ on earth, as beautiful and wonderful as that was, and as necessary as it was, could never bring us into the presence of God.

The only way that one could pass by the Veil, which pertained to the high priest only, was by the blood of sacrifice (Lev. 16:19). And yet, all of this gave testimony to the temporary nature of that dispensation. The very fact of the blood of the sacrifice, at the same time, stated that a perfect sacrifice was to come, which would open up the way to all. That perfect sacrifice, of course, was Christ on the Cross.

So, we might say, if the unrent Veil signified that the true way was not yet made known, it also implied that it would be made known.

All of this tells us that the sacrifice of Christ is the true ground of approach to God, and the true ground alone. His death, His blood, has opened up the way to His presence.

CUNNING WORK

The phrase, *"And fine twined linen of cunning work,"* tells us that this fabric was skillfully wrought. Literally, the Hebrew is, *"the work of a devisor."* This means that divine wisdom was given for its manufacture, and it was copied from a heavenly pattern, its equal never again being found on earth. It foreshadowed the humanity of our Lord, but yet, a humanity which was without sin.

Again I emphasize, because it's so very, very important, that His perfect humanity, and even His miracles, as necessary as they were, could not save anyone. That remained to be brought about by the Cross. But yet, this perfection was absolutely necessary, or else, the sacrifice could not be accepted. When we speak of *"perfection,"* we're speaking of sinless perfection. While there was no physical blemish on the body of Christ, there was no moral blemish, as well, on His soul. No other human being could say such a thing.

His divine birth, and it was divine, demanded that He be born of a virgin, i.e., *"the Virgin Mary."* Otherwise, He would have been born after Adam's fallen race, therefore, born into original sin as are all other human beings. However, Jesus was not born by the means of natural procreation, but rather by the decree of the Holy Spirit, which overshadowed Mary and brought about this miracle — and a miracle it was!

This means that Jesus did not carry any of the personality or physical traits of His foster father, or even His mother. In other words, Jesus was not the product of Joseph's seed or Mary's egg. In fact, she only provided a house for Him for the nine months of His gestation.

THE CHERUBIM AND THE COLORS: BLUE, PURPLE, AND SCARLET

CHERUBIM

The colors of *"blue, purple, and scarlet"* probably were incorporated in the embroidered Cherubim. The Cherubim emphasized the holiness of Christ and the fact that He was no less holy in His incarnate form than He had been in His form of deity. While He laid aside the expression of deity, He never for a moment lost possession of deity, hence, the holiness. Let's say it another way: As the Cherubim cry, *"Holy, Holy, Holy, Lord God Almighty,"* to God the Father, they say the same identical thing to God the Son, even though He was in incarnate form. The absolute holiness of His person diminished not at all!

THE SEDUCTION OF THE CHURCH

As the Scripture amply provides, which quickly becomes obvious, it is the Cross alone, as stated, which opened up the Veil (Mat. 27:51). Consequently, if the preacher is preaching the Gospel, He is preaching the Cross (I Cor. 1:18, 21, 23; 2:2; Col. 2:14-15; Gal. 6:14). If he's not preaching the Cross, while he may be preaching about the Gospel, he actually is not preaching the Gospel. Consequently, very few lives will be changed because the power of God is in the preaching of the Cross (I Cor. 1:17-18).

The Cross itself, and we are speaking of the wooden beam, contained no power, as would be obvious, and, in fact, the death of Christ contained no power either. Actually, the Scripture says, *"For though He was crucified through weakness, yet He lives by the power of God. For we also are weak in Him, but we shall live with Him by the power of God toward you."*

Paul continues, *"Examine yourselves, whether you be in the faith; prove your own selves. Know ye not your own selves how that Jesus Christ is in you, except you be reprobates?"* (II Cor. 13:4-5).

The power is in the Holy Spirit, as would be obvious! However, the Holy Spirit will not exhibit His power on our behalf, which is the source of all overcoming grace, except by and through the finished work of Christ. In fact, He cannot exhibit His power by any other means.

THE POWER OF THE HOLY SPIRIT

So, if the believer wants the power of the Holy Spirit, and I'm speaking of that power made real within our lives on a daily basis, even a constant basis, he can only have such by ever making the Cross of Christ the object of his faith (Rom. 8:2). In fact, the Lord Jesus Christ as the slain Lamb is forever intertwined, one might say, with the Holy Spirit, and the Holy Spirit with Christ in this manner (Rev. 5:6).

However, the church has been moved away from the Cross. Many forces have contributed to this present dilemma but, irrespective of the cause or the reason, the dirty deed has been done!

In the early church, and we specifically speak of the times of Paul, Satan used the Law/grace issue to hinder the preaching of the Cross; hence, almost all of Paul's 14 epistles were directed toward this difficulty and, in fact, were largely corrective.

Teachers whom Paul referred to as Satan's ministers (II Cor. 11:15) came into the churches built by the apostle and attempted to pull the people away from faith in the Cross toward Mosaic Law. To this effort, an effort engineered by Satan we might quickly add, the apostle strongly stated: *"But though we or an angel from Heaven preach any other Gospel unto you than that which we have preached unto you, let him be accursed"* (Gal. 1:8-9).

PREACHING THE CROSS

In effect, the apostle was saying that if the preacher is not preaching the Cross, then he's not preaching the Gospel and, in fact, is cursed by God and, as well, all who listen to such prattle are cursed by God. As I would hope is obvious, Paul's message was not a compromised message. In other words, it could not be compromised, and if it had been, you and I would not have the privilege of salvation at this present time.

In fact, God-called preachers aren't diplomats. They are supposed to be prophets, and they (we) are to deliver no less than *"thus saith the Lord!"*

The problem presently is not so much Law versus grace; although anything proposed other than the Cross must of necessity fall into the category of *"works"* in some way or fashion. The modern Word of Faith doctrine falls into that category and takes up where the Law/grace issue left off. In fact, in my personal opinion, it is far more lethal than the Law/grace problem because it's not as clear cut. In fact, millions follow this doctrine and really do not know what it teaches. One thing is for certain, the modern Word of Faith doctrine doesn't teach the Cross!

The Gospel of Jesus Christ is the Cross of Jesus Christ. One cannot read the writings of Paul, to whom was given the meaning of the New Covenant, which, in effect, is the meaning of the Cross, without coming to that conclusion.

So, the church, in one way or the other, has been pulled away from the Cross and is, therefore, powerless simply because the Holy Spirit will not function in that particular climate. Charles Solomon said, *"Since the vast majority of Christians do not understand the Cross experientially, the only other foundation on which to build their lives is the flesh, which is an inadequate undergirding for life and a Spirit-filled witness"* (I Cor. 3:11).

FOUR PILLARS

"And you shall hang it upon four pillars of shittim wood overlaid with gold: their hooks shall be of gold, upon the four sockets of silver" (Ex. 26:32).

As we shall see, five pillars stood at the front of the Tabernacle, while four pillars stood between the Holy Place and the Holy of Holies. The Veil was to be hung over these four pillars. The pillars were made of indestructible wood *"overlaid with gold,"* once again proclaiming the humanity of Christ as well as His deity.

The *"hooks"* were of pure gold and were evidently attached to the pillars. Considering that the Veil was attached to these hooks and covered the pillars, this tells us that the humanity and deity of Christ were but for one purpose, and that was to die on the Cross.

Inasmuch as there were four pillars, we have to assume that this represents the fourfold Gospel:

1. Salvation by the blood of Jesus.
2. The baptism with the Holy Spirit with the evidence of speaking with other tongues.
3. Divine healing.
4. The imminent return of our Lord to take away the true church in that which we refer to as the Rapture and, as well, the fact of Christ coming back to this earth to stay, i.e., *"the Second Coming."*

The fact that the four pillars were seated *"upon four sockets of silver"* speaks of redemption, which was the purpose of the Cross.

THE HOLY PLACE AND THE MOST HOLY

"And you shall hang up the veil under the taches, that you may bring in thither within the veil the Ark of the Testimony: And the veil shall divide unto you between the Holy Place and the Most Holy" (Ex. 26:33).

Once again, we remind the reader that the Veil was placed between the Holy Place and the Most Holy in order that entrance to the Most Holy would be barred. In fact, the whole ritual of Israel's worship emphasized the distance between God and fallen man. Bounds were set about Sinai so that not even a beast must touch it. One tribe alone was permitted to encamp immediately around the Tabernacle; that tribe was that of Levi. One family alone of that tribe was singled out and allowed to enter the Holy Place, and one man alone of that family had access into the Holiest, and that was only once a year. With such awe-inspiring preparation and ceremonies, it must have filled him with fear lest he should incur the judgment of the Most High.

As beautiful as was the Veil, it was not that beauty which made entrance possible, but rather the sprinkling of atoning blood before it! That beauty might be admired by the worshipper; he might sing hymns in its praise and give all sorts of sentimental and enduring names to it. He might use all kinds of poetic language in describing it. He might even copy it and produce similar patterns of embroidery or schemes of colors. But there was only one way of passing to the other side of it and of standing alive in the presence of God's glory and that was by sprinkling the blood before it and taking the blood of the victim beyond it. This blood told of substitution and acknowledged that he who entered did so as a sinner. By no other means could he stand on the other side of that Veil and live. He still says, *"When I see the blood, I will pass over you"* (Ex. 12:13).

THE FURNITURE OF THE HOLY PLACE

"And you shall put the Mercy Seat upon the Ark of the Testimony in the Most Holy Place.

"And you shall set the table without the veil, and the lampstand over against the table on the side of the Taber-

nacle toward the south: And you shall put the table on the north side" (Ex. 26:34-35).

In the Holy Place, we have the Lampstand on the south side, that is, the left side if one is standing facing the Tabernacle, with the Table of Shewbread on the opposite side, which would have been the north. Even though it's not mentioned here, the Altar of Incense would have sat immediately in front of the Veil in the Holy Place.

In effect, the Tabernacle was divided into three distinct parts:

1. *"The Court of the Tabernacle."* This was entered into through the gate in the fence at the front of the Tabernacle.
2. *"The Holy Place."*
3. *"The Holy of Holies where were the Ark of the Covenant and the Mercy Seat."*

The entrances into each of these were of the same materials — blue, purple, scarlet, and fine twined linen.

THE DOOR AND THE FIVE PILLARS

"And you shall make an hanging for the door of the tent, of blue, and purple, and scarlet, and fine twined linen, wrought with needlework.

"And you shall make for the hanging five pillars of shittim wood, and overlay them with gold, and their hooks shall be of gold: and you shall cast five sockets of copper for them" (Ex. 26:36-37).

The *"door of the tent"* led from the outside into the Holy Place. As well, there were several major differences.

The Veil had Cherubim embroidered upon it, while the door had none. The Veil, which separated the Holy Place from the Holy of Holies, was suspended from four pillars, while the door at the front of the Tabernacle was suspended from five. The four pillars had no "chapiters" on them, while the five pillars did. The sockets of the four were made of silver, while the sockets of the five were made of copper. However, the outstanding difference between them was this: *"the Veil was to shut out, whereas the door was to give admittance"*; the Veil barred the way into the Holiest; the door was for the constant entrance of the priests into the Holy Place.

THE DOOR AND THE FIVE PILLARS

As stated, the door, or gate one might say, was at the eastern end of the Tabernacle, which was the front. The door, or *"hanging,"* or gate, which gave admittance into the court of the Tabernacle, was not narrow, but rather stretched across the whole of its width, which was some 15 feet. It was also 15 feet high.

The fact that the Tabernacle faced the east carried with it a spiritual meaning as well.

In Genesis 3:24, we read that the Lord God *"drove out the man, and He placed at the east of the Garden of Eden Cherubims, and a flaming sword which turned every way, to keep the way of the Tree of Life."* We find from this that because of his sin, man was banished into darkness and at the east was stationed a flaming barrier. Here, however, there was a door or gate on the eastern side of the Tabernacle, which admitted men, after a fashion, into Jehovah's dwelling place!

THE NEEDLEWORK

Of the Veil, it is said that it was made *"of cunning work."* Of the door, the term is used, *"wrought with needlework."*

We must ever understand that there is nothing meaningless in Scripture. This means that there is a profound spiritual significance in everything that is stated. It's up to us to find out what it is.

"Needlework" is mentioned only in the description of the gate in the outer court (Ex. 27:16) and the girdle of the high priest (Ex. 28:39).

Looking at the Hebrew word rendered here *"needlework,"* it is also rendered *"the work of the embroiderer"* (Ex. 35:35), *"diverse colors"* (Ezek. 17:3), and in Psalms 139:15, it is translated *"curiously wrought."* Combining these slightly varied meanings, the term would denote *"minutely variegated."* Thus, it appears that the Holy Spirit here intimates that attention should be fixed upon the manner in which the different colors were wrought into and interwoven with the fine linen.

THE COLORS

Once again, we have the colors *"blue, and purple, and scarlet."* No less than 24 times is this combination repeated, yet never once is the order varied. This tells us something!

We know that everything in the Tabernacle pictured Christ in some manner as it regarded His atoning, mediatorial, and intercessory work.

It is said that if the blue and the scarlet were placed side by side without the intervention of some other color, the eye would be offended with the violet contrast. Though each is beautiful in itself and suitable to its own sphere, there is such a distinction, we might almost say opposition, in their hues as to render them inharmonious if seen in immediate contrast. However, the purple placed between the blue and the scarlet softens this impact. In fact, the purple is a mingling of both blue and scarlet.

So, we find that the scarlet and the blue are never placed in juxtaposition throughout the fabrics of the Tabernacle. Understanding that the Spirit of God is the one who has arranged this order, and seeing as to how He so minutely adhered to this order, we will now learn something about Christ which the Divine Spirit intends to teach.

WHAT THE HOLY SPIRIT INTENDS

The blue tells us from whence Christ has come, and we speak of heaven. The purple tells us of His royalty as king. The scarlet proclaims to us the price that He paid in order that fallen man might be saved. So, we learn that the one who died for us is a king, but not just any king, but rather the King from Glory, hence, the *"King of kings"* (Rev. 19:16).

Consequently, inasmuch as Christ is the King of kings, this speaks not only of His deity but, as well, of His *"finished work."* In other words, even though the plans for the Tabernacle were given some 1,500 years before Christ would come, in the mind of God there was no doubt that He would come and that He would accomplish the task at hand. He would go to the Cross, shed His life's blood, atone for all sin and, thereby, effect redemption for all who will believe (Jn. 3:16).

The term *"king"* is applied to Christ only as it regards His humanity and speaks of an accomplished work.

David is the man whom I personally believe was intended by God to be the first king of Israel. Saul was an aberration, the desire of the people and not the will of God; hence, his reign was anything but successful! He won some victories, even as the flesh will do, but couldn't win complete victory, even as the flesh cannot do. That remained for David to accomplish, which he did! David was placed on the throne by God, hence, God's choice. He would be the earthly type of the coming king, who, in fact, would be called, *"the Son of David"* (Mat. 1:1).

So, this one color, purple, placed between the blue and the scarlet tells us that the work for which Christ came from Heaven to accomplish would, in fact, be accomplished without fail!

FIVE PILLARS

There were five pillars at the front of the Tabernacle, whereas there were four, as stated, between the Holy Place and the Holy of Holies. They were made of indestructible wood, typifying, as also stated, the perfect humanity of Christ, and overlaid with gold, typifying His deity.

Hooks were placed on these five pillars, also of gold, in order to hold the *"door of the tent."*

The number five speaks of grace. For instance, Jesus had five names (Isa. 9:6); He suffered five wounds at His crucifixion: the nails in His hands, the nails in His feet, the spear in His side, the thorns on His brow, and the whip across His back. As well, David *"chose him five smooth stones out of the brook"* when he fought and defeated Goliath (I Sam. 17:40).

Whereas the *"sockets"* under the four pillars were of silver, signifying redemption, these sockets under the five pillars at the front of the Tabernacle were of brass, i.e., copper.

Brass, when used symbolically, prefigures judgment, which Jesus would endure at the Cross, all in our stead. Thus is the worshipper reminded once more that Christ is the door by reason of His sufferings in death. Pink said, and rightly so: *"May the Spirit of God ever keep before us the tremendous price which was paid to enable the Redeemed to come before God by sacrifices of praise and thanksgiving."*

> *"Jesus, plant and root in me*
> *"All the mind that was in Thee;*
> *"Settled peace I then shall find;*
> *"Jesus' is a quiet mind."*

"Anger I no more shall feel,
"Always even always still;
"Meekly on my God reclined
"Jesus' is a gentle mind."

"I shall suffer and fulfill
"All my Father's gracious will;
"Be in all alike resigned;
"Jesus' is a patient mind."

"When 'tis deeply rooted here,
"Perfect love shall cast out fear;
"Fear does servile spirits bind;
"Jesus' is a noble mind."

"I shall nothing know beside
"Jesus and Him crucified:
"Perfectly to Him be joined;
"Jesus' is a loving mind."

"Lowly, loving, meek and pure,
"I shall to the end endure:
"Be no more to sin inclined;
"Jesus' is a constant mind."

"I shall fully be restored
"To the image of my Lord;
"Witnessing to all mankind,
"Jesus' is a perfect mind."

5

The Brazen Altar

The Brazen Altar

"AND YOU SHALL make an altar of shittim wood, five cubits long, and five cubits broad; the altar shall be foursquare: and the height thereof shall be three cubits" (Ex. 27:1).

The Brazen Altar was the largest sacred vessel in the entirety of the seven vessels of the Tabernacle. It was seven and one-half feet long and seven and one-half feet wide. It was four and one-half feet high.

Going back to the *"cubits,"* the number *"five"* portrays the grace of God in sending His Son, the Lord Jesus Christ, who would suffer on our behalf. The number *"three,"* again respecting cubits but speaking of the height, refers to the deity of Christ.

Inasmuch as the altar was *"foursquare,"* this tells us that it is the same Gospel for all of mankind, whether north, south, east, or west. The problem is sin, and the solution is the Saviour. It doesn't matter what nationality the person might be, what race he might be, or whatever his status in society; the need is the same!

THE SAME GOSPEL FOR ALL

The church makes a terrible mistake when it tries to address the Gospel in a particular way to fit a particular people. When we read the book of Acts, which proclaims the manner in which the Holy Spirit carried out the work of God on earth through the apostles and others, we find that the same message was preached everywhere, irrespective of whom the people may have been. The message didn't change simply because the message didn't need to change. As stated, the problem is sin, irrespective as to whom the people might be, and the solution is the Saviour, and we might quickly say that the Saviour alone is the solution. Inasmuch as the Brazen Altar was the largest of all the sacred vessels, its size indicated its importance. As well, it was placed *"before the door"* (Ex. 40:6), just inside the outer court (Ex. 40:33), and would thus be the first object to meet the eye of the worshipper as he entered the fenced enclosure. It is designated *"the Brazen Altar"* (Ex. 38:30) to distinguish it from the *"Golden Altar."* It is also called *"the Altar of Burnt Offering"* (Ex. 30:28).

ITS SIGNIFICANCE

The altar typified Christ, and it typified what He would do in order to redeem humanity. Irrespective as to how one might try to dress it up, the Brazen Altar was a gruesome sight. The greasy smoke from the burning sacrifices constantly typified the judgment of God upon sin, and more specifically, upon an innocent victim, which was the lamb. This represented Christ and was not, to say the least, a pleasant sight to behold. There it stood: ever smoking, ever bloodstained, and ever open to any guilty Hebrew who might wish to approach it. For the sinner, having forfeited his life by sin, another life — one that was innocent — must be given in his stead.

In many ways, the Brazen Altar must be construed as the most important vessel designed by the Holy Spirit. Could it be more important than the Ark of the Covenant over which sat the Mercy Seat? This represented the Holy of Holies, typifying the very throne of God! However, no one could reach that place and position except by the Brazen Altar, which typified Calvary. I would have to say that the Cross of Christ stands supreme at the very intersection of humanity and, as well, of Heaven itself. Concerning this, Paul said: **"That in the dispensation of the fullness of times, He** (*God the Father*) **might gather together in one all things in Christ, both which are in Heaven and which are on the earth; even in Him"** (Eph. 1:10).

The phrase, *"in Christ,"* speaks entirely of the Cross, and, as well, this verse tells us that the Cross addressed itself not only to fallen man but to the revolution led by Satan in eternity past. This is proven by the word *"Heaven."* So, if we want to try to put a label on these all-important things, I think we can safely say that the Cross stands at the intersection of both Heaven and earth. It is impossible, I think, to overemphasize the Cross, while very much possible to minimize its significance.

THE HORNS

"And you shall make the horns of it upon the four corners thereof: his horns shall be of the same, and you shall overlay it with copper" (Ex. 27:2).

The altar of indestructible wood was to be *"overlaid with copper."*

Until the metallurgy of the not-two-distant past, copper had a greater resistance to fire even than gold or silver. Consequently, it would protect the wood that it would not catch fire and be consumed. Pink said, *"As the copper plates on the altar protected it from the fervent heat and prevented it from being burned up, so Christ passed through the fires of God's wrath without being consumed. He is mighty to save, because He was mighty to endure."*

In Scripture, *"copper"* symbolizes judgment. This is the reason that Moses was instructed to make *"a serpent of copper"* and place it on a pole. The Children of Israel, who had been bitten by serpents, were instructed to look at this copper serpent, and upon looking, they would be healed (Num. 21:8).

THE SERPENT ON THE POLE

The serpent on the pole symbolized Christ on the Cross; consequently, many have wondered why the Holy Spirit would have used a serpent made of copper as a symbol of the perfect, untainted, and unsullied Son of God. They can understand a dove, but a serpent? Surely this would be the last of all objects suited to portray Him who is fairer than the children of men!

No, it wasn't a mistake. The serpent was the only symbol which could properly portray what would be carried out on the Cross. The serpent was the reminder of the curse (Gen., Chpt. 3), and in Galatians 3:13, we are expressly told that Christ was *"made a curse"* for His people.

As well, the serpent that Moses was instructed to make at that particular time was to be of copper and not of silver or of gold because it was to represent Jesus suffering the judgment of God on the Cross.

On the Cross, Jesus would atone for all sin, thereby, defeating that old serpent called *"the Devil."* It was at the Cross where sin was addressed, where Satan and all his cohorts of darkness were defeated. So, the serpent on the pole symbolized what Jesus would there do, and which He did do.

THE AWFULNESS OF SIN

In both the Brazen Altar and the Brazen Serpent, we see the awfulness of sin. We see that it is so horrible, so deadly, so degrading, and so destructive that even though God could speak worlds into existence, He could not speak redemption into existence and continue to be true to His nature. Sin and all of its effects had to be addressed, and the only way it could be addressed was for the price to be paid regarding atonement. No man could pay that price, so God Himself would have to pay that which was owed.

This means that man has absolutely no argument left. If God had demanded that man pay the price, perhaps man might have an argument; however, God would pay the price, and at frightful cost. In fact, we learn how bad sin is by the price that was paid in order for sin to be assuaged.

What Jesus did on the Cross not only addressed the effects of sin, which means it atoned for the terrible ravages of sin, but He also addressed the cause of sin. This Jesus did by the shedding of His precious blood. The cause of sin is twofold.

THE CAUSE OF SIN

All sin stems from Satan himself, the archenemy of God. It has as its receptacle the evil hearts of men. That's the reason that it's impossible to address sin by addressing the environment, education, economic structure, or social rehabilitation. Those things only address symptoms and not at all the cause. The cause, as far as man is concerned, is Satan himself, who functions through the evil heart of man, which was brought about as a result of the Fall. In other words, sin comes from within, which means that man has no solution for this terrible problem.

However, when Jesus died on the Cross, He atoned for all sin — past, present, and future — at least for all who will believe. This totally and completely defeated Satan and all of his evil cohorts, and did so by removing the legal right that the Evil One had to hold man in bondage.

That's why Paul said: **"And having spoiled principalities and powers** (*Satan and his minions*)**, He made a show of them openly, triumphing over them in it"** **(Col. 2:15).** He did this by and through what He did at the Cross.

THE CONQUERING OF SIN

My next statement will be somewhat shocking because it flies in the face of the thinking of most Christians. Let us proceed: there is nothing in the Bible that even remotely mentions the fact that believers must conquer sin! The truth is, sin has already been conquered by Jesus Christ, as it could only be conquered by Jesus Christ. When we try to conquer it ourselves, we are, in effect, saying that what Christ did at the Cross was insufficient and must have our contribution in order for His work to be complete.

Such an idea borders on blasphemy! However, this is where most modern Christians are, albeit ignorantly!

Most Christians do not understand the cause of sin in their lives, and please remember, we're speaking here of true Christians, those who truly love God. So, when they fail the Lord, almost invariably, the Christian addresses the symptoms instead of the real cause.

Let us state it again: most of the time, one doesn't address the cause simply because one doesn't know or understand the cause. Consequently, the lives of most Christians play out to a constant struggle, with them losing this struggle most of the time. In other words, Satan is overcoming them, and they are perpetually failing the Lord in some way.

Why?

GOD'S PRESCRIBED ORDER OF VICTORY

The Christian fails the Lord, in other words, he sins in some way because he is rebelling against God's prescribed order of victory. With some, it is a deliberate rebellion, while with others, it is rebellion because of ignorance of this prescribed order. Either way though, hurt and harm will be the result.

God's prescribed order of victory is the Cross of Christ, through and by which the Holy Spirit works (Rom. 8:1-2, 11). One must understand, there is only one solution for sin, only one, and that is the Cross of Christ (Heb. 10:12-14).

The Christian is to understand that Jesus won a complete victory at the Cross, atoning for all sin, thereby, defeating the powers of darkness in their totality. His work was a finished work.

This means that whatever sin, iniquity, or transgression with which Satan would approach the child of God, it has already been addressed at the Cross. Satan is able to peddle his wares only because the Christian doesn't understand who he really is in Christ.

THE CROSS

The Christian must, without fail, understand that his victory is totally and completely in the Cross of Christ. It was there that the price was paid, there that victory was won, and there that all sin was atoned. When we sing the song, "Jesus Paid It All," it means exactly what it says!

It would seem, would it not, that what we've just said is very, very simple and not hard at all to understand. In fact, it is simple! Actually, it is not hard to understand! So, the problem is not theological, but rather moral. What do I mean by that?

In order for the Christian to put his faith totally and completely in Christ and what Christ has done for him at the Cross, he has to overcome two obstacles.

NO CONFIDENCE IN THE CROSS

He will soon find out that most of the church world, and it probably includes where he presently attends church, while they pay lip service to the Cross, in effect, place little confidence in the Cross. This is proven by the crises that arise in the church. In other words, if failure is enjoined, it is seldom that the Cross is recommended as the solution, but rather the psychological way. In fact, the far greater majority of the modern church will not even accept the victory and deliverance that comes through the Cross. They demand a sign-off by a psychologist. So, the whole tenor of the church militates against the Cross. In fact, the Cross of Christ is the dividing line between the true church and the apostate church.

So, the believer, and especially the preacher, is going to have to understand that when he places his faith and trust exclusively in Christ and what He did at the Cross, which then gives the Holy Spirit latitude to work mightily within his life, he will probably be ostracized by the far greater majority of the modern church. Regrettably, most aren't willing to pay that price. Never mind that there is no victory whatsoever in the direction of the apostate church; most Christians simply cannot buck the tide.

THE PROBLEM OF SELF

There is something in us, even the most consecrated, that wants to try to believe that whatever it is we are facing, we can handle it ourselves. In other words, even though everybody else has failed, *"I can do it"* seems to be the attitude of most all of us.

However, the truth is, you can't do it. Why?

The believer must understand that in living this life for the Lord, we are facing more than just an emotional problem, etc. The believer is facing the powers of darkness, beginning with Satan, then to fallen angels, and then to demon spirits. That's why Paul said, *"For we wrestle not against flesh and blood, but against principalities, against powers, against the rulers of the darkness of this world, against spiritual wickedness in high places"* (Eph. 6:12).

The great apostle also told us, *"For though we walk in the flesh, we do not war after the flesh, for the weapons of our warfare are not carnal, but mighty through God to the pulling down of strongholds"* (II Cor. 10:3-4).

If it is to be noticed, the great apostle used words such as *"war"* and *"warfare,"* which means this is something very, very serious. It doesn't matter that we are saved and baptized with the Holy Spirit and totally sincere before the Lord, within ourselves, we are no match for these powers of darkness. Some would instantly retort, *"But I'm not trying to do this myself; the Holy Spirit is helping me."* Most definitely, the Holy Spirit is the answer, but how is He the answer?

HOW THE HOLY SPIRIT WORKS

The Holy Spirit is God, meaning that He can do anything; however, He will not force Himself on us. He doesn't require much of us, but He does require one definite thing, and that is the following:

The Holy Spirit works exclusively within the framework of the finished work of Christ, i.e., the Cross.

Paul said, *"The Law of the Spirit of Life in Christ Jesus has made me free from the Law of sin and death"* (Rom. 8:2).

This means that there is only one thing that is stronger than the *"Law of sin and death,"* and that is *"the Law of the Spirit of Life in Christ Jesus."* The short phrase, "in Christ Jesus," which Paul used approximately 170 times in one form or the other in his 14 epistles, refers to what Jesus Christ did at the Cross.

So, the Holy Spirit demands that the object of our faith be the Cross of Christ (Rom. 6:1-14; 8:1-11; I Cor. 1:17-18, 23; 2:2; Gal. 6:14; Col. 2:10-15). In fact, every single sacrifice offered up in Old Testament times represented and symbolized Jesus Christ and what He would do for us at the Cross.

With our faith anchored totally and completely in Christ and what Christ has done for us at the Cross, the Holy Spirit will then do great and mighty things for us. If our faith is placed in anything else, the Holy Spirit looks at it as *"spiritual adultery"* (Rom. 7:1-4). As adultery causes extreme trouble in a marriage, as would be obvious, likewise, spiritual adultery has the same effect in our living for God. In other words, when we look to anything other than the Cross of Christ, we are being unfaithful to Christ, which the Holy Spirit labels as spiritual adultery (Rom. 7:4).

But yet, it is hard for Christians to admit all of this. We are loath to give up our little pet stratagems in favor of living a life totally dependent on Christ and what He did for us at the Cross. However, there is victory in no other means or methods than the Cross. The Cross alone provides what we must have, and, of course, we speak of the benefits of the Cross, and that scriptural truth will never change.

The Cross of Christ is God's prescribed order of victory. He has no other because He needs no other.

ALL THE GLORY TO GOD

The Cross of Christ is the only thing that gives all glory to the Lord. With anything and everything else that the believer might try to do to get victory over sin, if there is a tiny bit of victory, the glory goes to the individual and not the Lord. That's why Paul said, **"God forbid, that I should glory** (*boast*) **save in the Cross of our Lord Jesus Christ, by whom the world is crucified unto me, and I unto the world" (Gal. 6:14).**

THE BINDING OF THE SACRIFICE

The horns, which were on each corner of the Brazen Altar and pointing outward, were for the binding of the sacrifice to the altar (Ps. 118:27). In Scripture, the horn stands for power and strength (Hab. 3:4).

One might say that it was not the nails which held Christ to the Cross, but rather the unfaltering purpose of the Saviour and the strength of His love.

While on the Cross, His enemies challenged Him to come down; His refusal to do so evidenced the cords which bound Him to its *"horns."*

THE ASHES

"And you shall make his pans to receive his ashes, and his shovels, and his basons, and his fleshhooks, and his firepans: All the vessels thereof you shall make of copper" (Ex. 27:3).

Pink said, *"Ashes testified to the thoroughness of the fires' work in having wholly consumed the offering. They also witnessed to the acceptance of the sacrifice on behalf of the offerer, and so they were to him a token that his sins were gone. The words of Christ from the Cross express the fulfillment of this detail of our type: 'It is finished' announced that the Sacrifice had been offered, accepted, and gone up to God as a sweet savor."*

THE ASHES, SHOVELS, BASONS, FLESHHOOKS, AND FIREPANS

As it regards the various utensils, all designed by the Holy Spirit we might quickly add, all played their part as it regarded the sacrifice being offered up properly.

When it comes to the crucifixion of Christ, the Scripture says, *"How much more shall the blood of Christ, who through the Eternal Spirit offered Himself without spot to God"* (Heb. 9:14).

This means that the Holy Spirit planned every detail of the death of the Son of God, even down to the moment when He would tell Him that He could die. Ever let it be understood that Jesus was not executed. Even though such was in the murderous hearts of those who demanded His crucifixion, He, in fact, laid down His life freely. In other words, no one took it from Him (Jn. 10:17-18).

That all were made of copper emphasizes again the prominent and dominant truth associated with this altar — the unsparing judgment of God upon the believing sinner's substitute.

THE GRATE ON THE BRAZEN ALTAR

"And you shall make for it a grate of network of copper; and upon the net shall you make four copper rings in the four corners thereof.

"And you shall put it under the compass of the altar beneath, that the net may be even to the midst of the altar" (Ex. 27:4-5).

The altar was hollow, although, after the Temple was built and it became a fixed object, more than likely, it was filled up with earth, with the *"grate"* over the top. However, during the wilderness experience, it is almost certain that it remained hollow to make it easier to move, which it sometimes was.

The *"grate of network of copper"* provided a top for the altar on which the parts of the animals were laid. The *"network"* was held up by *"four copper rings in the four corners."*

Somewhere alongside the middle of the altar, there seemed to be a protrusion all the way around on which the priests could stand in order to properly attend to the sacrifices.

In a sense, this grate symbolized the wooden beam to which Jesus was nailed.

THE STAVES

"And you shall make staves for the altar, staves of shittim wood, and overlay them with copper.

"And the staves shall be put into the rings, and the staves shall be upon the two sides of the altar, to bear it.

"Hollow with boards shall you make it: As it was shewed you in the mount, so shall they make it" (Ex. 27:6-8).

THE STAVES

The entire camp of Israel often moved while in the wilderness; consequently, everything had to be moved, as would be obvious. The Brazen Altar was carried by staves, teaching the lesson that there never comes a period in the Christian life where the atoning blood of Christ can be dispensed with. But yet, and tragically so, this is exactly what most modern Christians do. After the initial salvation experience, they leave the Cross for other things, thereby, placing their faith in other things, which is the cause of all spiritual tragedy.

THE CROSS AND SANCTIFICATION

As the believing sinner must look to Christ and the Cross as it regards the initial salvation experience, likewise, the believer must continue to look to the Cross as it regards sanctification. In other words, the Cross of Christ plays the signal part in every aspect of the believer's experience, irrespective as to what it might be. However, tragically, most Christians don't know this.

Because of having so little teaching on the subject, after conversion, many, if not most, Christians attempt to live for God in all the wrong ways. While there are any number of wrong ways, there's only one right way, and that is for the believer to continue to look to Christ and the Cross for all things, irrespective as to what they might be. The believer must ever place his or her faith in the finished work of Christ, never allowing it to be moved to other things. This then gives the Holy Spirit, as previously stated, the latitude to work as only the Holy Spirit can work (Rom. 8:1-2, 11).

When the priests burned incense on the Golden Altar (actually the Altar of Incense), which they did twice a day, morning and evening, coals of fire were taken from the Brazen Altar each time and placed on the Golden Altar, with incense poured over these coals. This signified that all intercession by Christ, along with the presentation of our praises, is made possible by what Christ did at the Cross. In other words, Christ is making intercession for us in Heaven at this very moment due to the fact of what He did at the Cross on our behalf. So, unless one understands the Cross, one cannot understand much of anything carried out by Christ.

"Lord Jesus, I long to be perfectly whole.
"I want You forever to live in my soul;
"Break down every idol, cast out every foe
"Now wash me, and I shall be whiter than snow."

"Lord Jesus, let nothing unholy remain,
"Apply Your own blood and extract every stain;
"To get this blest cleansing I all things forego,
"Now wash me, and I shall be whiter than snow."

"Lord Jesus, look down from Your throne in the skies,
"And help me to make a complete sacrifice;
"I give up myself and whatever I know —
"Now wash me, and I shall be whiter than snow."

"Lord Jesus, for this I most humbly entreat,
"I wait, blessed Lord, at Your crucified feet;
"By faith for my cleansing I see Your blood flow,
"Now wash me, and I shall be whiter than snow."

6

The Brazen Laver

CHAPTER SIX

The Brazen Laver

"AND THE LORD spoke unto Moses, saying,
"You shall also make a laver of copper, and his foot also
of copper, to wash withal: and you shall put it between
the Tabernacle of the congregation, and the altar (Brazen
Altar)*, and you shall put water therein"* (Ex. 30:17-18).

Whereas the Brazen Altar was made of indestructible
wood and overlaid with copper, the *"laver"* was made of
nothing but copper. (Even though the King James transla-
tors used the word *"brass,"* it should have been translated
"copper" simply because brass is a mixture of metals, of
which such metallurgy was not known at that time. The original text did not use the word *"brass."*)

Measurements for all of the vessels were given, with the
exception of the Brazen Laver and the Golden Lampstand.
The Brazen Altar had rings and staves for carrying it; the laver
had none. The Brazen Altar was to be covered when Israel
journeyed, but nothing is said of this regarding the laver. The
altar was for fire; the laver for water.

CLEANSING FROM DAILY DEFILEMENT

The Brazen Laver sat between the Brazen Altar and the Tabernacle, thereby, stating by its very presence that cleansing from daily defilement had to be engaged by the priests before they entered the Tabernacle, no matter how many times they entered. The laver alone, which was a type of the Word of God, was able to effect such cleansing. The idea is this, at least as it regards modern believers: it is the Word of God of which the laver was a type, which tells us what is right and what is wrong and how we can be cleansed from all wrong. The laver testified that the believer doesn't have to get saved over and over again but that cleansing can be effected on a daily basis, even an hourly basis, by the Word of God. It tells us what to do, which the next few verses proclaim, and that cleansing will be effected. One might say that the Brazen Altar was for the sinner and the Brazen Laver for the saint. The former testified of the blood of Christ; the latter of the Word of God. The former cleansed the conscience, at least as best that the altar could cleanse such; the latter, the Brazen Laver, the conduct.

WATER AND NOT BLOOD

If it is to be noticed, water and not blood was to be the element appointed and used for the purification of the priests. It was plainly a figure of the written Word of God. The Psalmist said, *"Wherewithal shall a young man cleanse his way? By taking heed thereto according to Your word"* (Ps. 119:9). Jesus said, *"Now you are clean through the word which I have spoken unto you"* (Jn. 15:3). The disciples didn't need to be saved, that having already been accomplished, but they definitely needed cleansing on a constant basis, as we shall shortly see.

THE WASHING

"*For Aaron and his sons shall wash their hands and their feet thereat:*
"*When they go into the Tabernacle of the congregation, they shall wash with water, that they die not; or when they come near to the altar to minister, to burn offerings made by fire unto the LORD:*

THE WASHING

"So they shall wash their hands and their feet that they die not: and it shall be a statute forever to them, even to him and to his seed throughout their generations" (Ex. 30:19-21).

The Brazen Altar and the Brazen Laver must not be confused; and yet, I am concerned that they are repeatedly confused with many, if not most, Christians.

Verse 19 tells us that Aaron and his sons had to wash their hands and their feet every time they went into the Tabernacle to perform their duties, no matter how many the times. However, they didn't have to offer up a lamb every time they did this. The Brazen Altar was a figure of regeneration; the Brazen Laver typified the Christian's need of daily cleansing.

We have a portrayal of this in John, Chapter 13. It is the example of Jesus washing the feet of the disciples.

As Jesus began to wash the feet of the disciples, Peter said to Him, *"You shall never wash my feet."* The answer of our Lord was very cryptic. He said, *"If I wash you not, you have no part with Me."*

Then Peter, in typical fashion, answered, *"Lord, not my feet only, but also my hands and my head."*

Jesus said to him, *"He who is washed needs only to wash his feet"* (Jn. 13:8-10).

THE FEET AND THE HANDS

The Exodus text tells us that the priests had to wash both their hands and their feet, but Jesus says here that it is only the feet that need to be washed. Why the difference?

Christ wasn't attempting to institute an ordinance, which some have tried to claim. Some have thought that a foot-washing service denoted humility and should, thereby, be carried out on a regular basis. That's not what Jesus was teaching.

The book of Acts is an account of the early church. While Paul did mention the washing of the feet of the saints by widows in the book of Acts, he wasn't speaking of an ordinance, but rather of service being rendered and performed, in other words, making oneself useful (I Tim. 5:10). To make an ordinance out of this takes us back to the Law, which Jesus has fulfilled, and which we must not do.

Jesus mentioned only the feet, while the priests, as stated, had to wash both hands and feet. The reason follows.

DOING

The hands signify *"doing"* and, in Christ, relative to what He did at the Cross, all has been done. So, to wash the hands, symbolically speaking, would, in effect, state that Christ hadn't paid the price, etc.

As is obvious, the feet are symbolic of our daily walk before the Lord. It concerns our everyday living, in other words, how we order our behavior. Considering that we are living in a defiled world, mixing with unbelievers who are perpetually defiled, it states that our *"walk,"* symbolized by the feet, must ever be corrected and cleansed. This is done by a constant application of the Word of God, which keeps us walking in a straight path and, as well, cleanses our walk.

THE WORD OF GOD

The mere reading of the Word, although necessary, is not enough within itself. We must understand what it means and then apply it to our hearts and lives, which the Holy Spirit will definitely do if we are sincere before the Lord.

Just having the Brazen Laver there was not enough within itself. The priests had to wash constantly, and this speaks of every time they went into the Tabernacle, showing the constant need. That's one of the reasons that Jesus said that we must take up our Cross daily (Lk. 9:23).

In effect, the Brazen Laver showed the priests the effect that the Brazen Altar had on their lives. The altar was a symbol of the covenant, which was sealed in blood, typified by the slain lamb.

The Word (Brazen Laver) now tells me constantly what the great sacrifice of Christ means to me, and means to me on a daily, even minute-by-minute basis. The understanding provided by the Word cleanses my walk and, as well, keeps it straight. Unless that water (Word) is applied on a constant basis, the results will not be pleasant.

SPIRITUAL DEATH

"They shall wash with water, that they die not" (Ex. 30:20).

I should think that we ought to understand that we're dealing with something here that is very serious.

Let us understand that no dimensions were given as it regards the size of the laver. I'm sure the Lord gave a particular size to Moses, according to which the laver would be constructed, but Moses didn't give it to us. Why?

The idea is twofold:

1. There was a constant need for the laver, even as there is a constant need for the Word.

2. It doesn't really matter how dirty the feet and the hands of the priests became, there was to be enough water to accomplish the task, which demanded that the laver be constantly replenished. This is the reason no size or dimension is given to us.

If the priests didn't follow the command concerning constant washings as given by the Lord, they could be stricken dead. It is the same presently.

If believers ignore what the Word of God tells us as it regards cleansing respecting our daily walk, spiritual death can definitely be the result.

THE CROSS IS THE DIVIDING LINE

Through this ministry and others, the Lord is making plain and clear the Message of the Cross (I Cor. 1:17-18, 21, 23; 2:2, 5). Constant faith in the Cross, to which the Word clearly points us, is demanded, or else, as stated, spiritual death will be the result.

This means that the church must heed what Paul taught, which is the meaning of the New Covenant, which is the meaning of the Cross, which is the Gospel (I Cor. 1:17).

Satan has been very successful in the last few decades at pushing the church away from the Cross. Actually, it began with the Pentecostal world in the late 1950s. The church began to dabble with humanistic psychology until now (2014), when humanistic psychology is being embraced in totality. You cannot have both the Cross of Christ and humanistic psychology. Either one cancels out the other. As a result, the modern church little knows where it's been, where it is, or where it's going. False doctrine is rampant and getting worse! The answer to all of this is the Cross of Christ and the Cross of Christ alone.

THE LIGHT

If this *"light"* is rejected, spiritual death will be the result. This will play out to spiritual wreckage, which has already begun. Most modern Christians have little idea as to how to live a godly life. In fact, the subject is rarely broached anymore from behind modern pulpits. If it is mentioned, the poor people are mostly given the wrong instructions. In other words, they are directed to *"Law,"* which only tends to exacerbate the problem. Most Christians live a life of spiritual failure, with some of them trying hard not to do so, but it seems the harder they try, the worse the situation becomes. Why?

Even though their motives and intentions are good, they are trying to do something which, in the first place, Christ has already done, and which they cannot do anyway. The Brazen Laver (the Word) alone holds the answer to their dilemma, but regrettably and sadly, they don't understand the Word.

The Cross of Christ, to which the Word directs us (Rom. 6:3-14; 8:1-2, 11; Eph. 2:13-18; Col. 2:10-15), is the dividing line between the true church and the apostate church. Let's look at that a little closer.

INSTITUTIONALIZED RELIGION

I was asked the other day to define institutionalized religion. The explanation is this: it is the part of the church world, which incorporates almost all, that has as the object of its faith something other than the Cross. In other words, the people are directed toward the particular denomination or toward a doctrine which is unbiblical. That is the difference.

I do not mean to say that every religious denomination in the world presents as the object of faith something other than the Cross. However, I do know that most in the United States and Canada fall into that category. For the most part, the situation comes to the place of spiritual disaster slowly; consequently, the people are somewhat like a frog placed in a pot of water, with the pot then placed over the fire. The water heats up slowly, so slowly, in fact, that the frog little notices it until it's too late. In other words, it acclimates itself to the changing temperature until finally, the water is boiling and the frog dies. It is the same with believers. Things change slowly, so slowly, in fact, that the change is difficult to notice, but then spiritual death starts taking place all around them, and many wonder as to the cause.

EXAMINE YOURSELVES

The believer had better inspect minutely what is the object of his faith. Paul said, *"Examine yourselves, whether you be in the faith; prove your own selves. Know ye not your own selves, how that Jesus Christ is in you, except you be reprobates?"* (II Cor. 13:5).

Each person claiming Christ had better take a minute inventory of the church with which he or she is involved, irrespective as to what it is. Is the Cross of Christ being preached? That means the Cross of Christ must ever be the object of our faith!

If other things are being touted, such a believer had best seek the Lord earnestly about changing churches. The believer is by and large going to be what he hears preached from behind the pulpit, whatever that pulpit might be. That needs qualification!

If error is being preached, and the person continues to listen to such error, he will ultimately become that error. It is inevitable! However, if the truth is being preached, even if the person constantly hears the truth, it doesn't necessarily hold that he will heed that truth. The opportunity is present, but regrettably, all do not heed. That's why Jesus constantly said, *"He who has ears to hear, let him hear"* (Mat. 11:15; 13:9, 43; Mk. 4:9).

Faith is the key (Gal. 5:6), but it must be faith in the correct object, and that object must be the Cross of Christ, which, in effect, is the story in totality of the Word of God (I Cor. 1:17; Col. 2:10-15).

A BRIEF SUMMARY OF THE GOSPEL

What we are about to give you is an abbreviation of the Gospel, actually, a gross abbreviation; however, if you will look at it closely, I think you will find that it adheres totally to the Word of God. It is the solution and the only solution.

- Jesus Christ is the source of all things that we receive from God (Jn. 1:1-3, 14, 29; Col. 2:10-15).
- The Cross of Christ is the means and the only means by which all of these wonderful things are given to us (Rom. 6:1-14; I Cor. 1:17-18, 23).
- Considering that Jesus is the source, and the Cross is the means, then the object of our faith must always be Christ and the Cross (I Cor. 2:2; Gal. 6:14).

- With our faith in the correct object, which is the Cross of Christ, the Holy Spirit, who works exclusively within the boundaries, so to speak, of the finished work of Christ, will then work mightily on our behalf. He doesn't demand much of us, but He most definitely does demand that the object of our faith ever be the Cross, else we are functioning in spiritual adultery, which greatly hinders the Holy Spirit, as should be obvious (Rom. 8:1-11; Eph. 2:13-18).

Most of the church world, and we speak of those who at least maintain a semblance of orthodoxy, will have no problem understanding that Jesus is the source of all things we receive from God. However, it's the second point where the problem comes in.

When we state that the Cross of Christ is the *"means"* by which we receive all of these good things, that becomes a sticking point for many Christians. People like to believe that whatever it is they are doing, no matter how wrong it might be, it is the answer and solution for which they seek. However, there is only one answer and only one solution, and that is *"Jesus Christ and Him crucified."*

Arguing about whether the Cross is the means and the only means, it is then easy for the believer to place his or her faith in something else, such as fasting, witnessing, etc. In fact, the list is long! However, what we fail to realize is, if we have anything as the object of our faith other than *"Christ crucified,"* we are constituted by the Lord as living in a state of spiritual adultery (Rom. 7:1-5). One can well imagine how much this hinders the Holy Spirit. Thank God that He doesn't leave us, but still, adopting such a course, and we speak of that which is other than the Cross, greatly hinders the Spirit, which is the reason for so much failure.

Whether we realize it or not, sin is the problem, and the only answer for sin is the Cross of Christ (Heb. 10:12).

THE STORY OF THE BIBLE

The entirety of the story of the Word of God, and we're speaking of everything from Genesis through the book of Revelation, is *"Jesus Christ and Him crucified."* So, when one has his faith anchored squarely in the Cross of Christ, he in actuality has his faith in the Word. When we speak of the Cross, we aren't speaking of the wooden beam on which Jesus died, but rather what He there accomplished. He came to this world to go to the Cross, and that He did, and there He accomplished all He came to do.

"For God so loved the world, that He gave His only begotten Son, that whosoever believes in Him, should not perish, but have everlasting life" (Jn. 3:16).

"Give me a sight, O Saviour,
"Of Your wondrous love to me,
"Of the love that brought You down to earth,
"To die on Calvary."

"Was it the nails, O Saviour,
"That bound You to the tree?
"No, 'twas Your everlasting love,
"Your love for me, for me."

"O, wonder of all wonders,
"That through Your death for me,
"My open sins, my secret sins,
"Can all forgiven be."

"Then melt my heart O Saviour,
"Bend me, yea break me down,
"Until I own You conqueror,
"And Lord and Sovereign crown."

7

The Table of Shewbread

CHAPTER SEVEN

The Table of Shewbread

"YOU SHALL ALSO make a table of shittim wood: two cubits shall be the length thereof, and a cubit the breadth thereof, and a cubit and a half the height thereof" (Ex. 25:23).

This Table was made of indestructible wood, which, as stated, pictured and proclaimed the perfect humanity of Christ. The Table was 36 inches long, 18 inches wide, and 27 inches high.

The Holy Spirit through Moses now takes us into the Holy Place, separated from the Holy of Holies by a Veil.

In the Holy of Holies, the high priest ministered only one day a year, the Great Day of Atonement. In the Holy Place, the regular priests, one might say, ministered daily. In the Holy Place stood three pieces of sacred furniture. If you were walking through the front door, to your left would be the Golden Lampstand, to the right would be the Table of Shewbread, which we are now studying, and immediately in front of the Veil in the center would be the Altar of Incense.

Considering that the Altar of Incense is the first of the sacred vessels that one would see coming out of the Holy of Holies, one would think that this would be the next one named; however, the Holy Spirit, as is obvious here, rather deals first with the Table of Shewbread. When we see the meaning of the Table, we shall then see why the Holy Spirit has pointed it out first. No regular Israelite could enter into the Holy Place or the Holy of Holies. None but the priestly family ever penetrated this sacred precinct. Under the old economy, all priests were types of Christ, with the high priest of Israel being the greatest type of all.

However, presently, through what Jesus has done for us at the Cross, every saint of God, no matter who the person might be or where the person might be, is now a member of the *"chosen generation, a royal priesthood"* (I Pet. 2:9).

THE PURPOSE OF THE TABLE

The shewbread consisted of 12 loaves, made of fine flour, baked and placed in two rows upon the table. Those loaves were to remain there for seven days, and then they were eaten by the priests.

This is typical of Jesus as the Bread of Life. Thus, the Holy Spirit reveals the sufficiency of Christ as the bread of His people day-by-day and always fresh.

As the number *"seven"* speaks of the perfection of Christ, which, as well, speaks of the perfection of His work, the number *"12"* speaks of His perfect government.

Under the Law, the perfection of Christ could not be totally revealed, while under grace, it is most definitely revealed in totality. The priests of old could only eat the bread on the seventh day, while we partake of Christ presently on a daily basis.

In effect, this is what Christ was speaking about when He said, *"As the Living Father has sent Me, and I live by the Father: so he who eats Me, even he shall live by Me"* (Jn. 6:57).

THE CROSS

The way that we *"eat Christ,"* and do so on a daily basis, is by trusting Him, which refers to trusting what He did at the Cross on our behalf.

To explain it even further, Jesus also said, *"If any man will come after Me, let him deny himself, and take up his Cross daily and follow Me"* (Lk. 9:23).

As stated, the 12 loaves signify the government of God, as the number 12 always signifies such as it relates to the Lord. As should be understood, there is nothing more important for the believer than an understanding of God's government, which means to understand His ways. In this way alone can we have life and victory.

To understand His government, one must first understand the Cross. Without properly understanding the Cross and what it actually means, it is impossible to understand God's government.

COMMUNION

In Verse 22, the Lord mentioned *"Communion,"* and the Table, which He addresses next, speaks of Communion as well. In I Corinthians, Chapter 10, Paul taught us that the table is inseparably connected with Communion. He refers to it as *"the Lord's table,"* which is always symbolic of fellowship with Christ. Pink said: *"We learn that the blood-sprinkled*

Mercy Seat speaks of Christ as the 'basis' of our fellowship with God, while the Table points to Christ as the 'substance' of that fellowship." He then went on to say, *"The Table sets forth Jehovah's feast of love for His saints and for Himself in fellowship with them."*

THE DIMENSIONS OF THE TABLE

We find that the Table, although the same height as the Ark, yet fell short of its length and width.

This tells us that it is impossible to exhaust Christ. No matter how much we partake of Him, we always fall short of exhausting His potential.

We can say the same thing as it regards the Cross. Whatever the Lord shows us about the Cross, however deep it might be, we will shortly find that we have not exhausted its potential, and neither is it possible to exhaust its potential. That's why Paul referred to the Cross as *"the Everlasting Covenant"* (Heb. 13:20).

In 1997, when the Lord first began to show me the meaning of the Cross as it refers to the believer's sanctification, I sensed in my spirit that as grand and as glorious as those beginning days were, still, I was only scratching the surface, so to speak. In seeking the Lord and sensing in my spirit, as the Holy Spirit revealed it to me, that it was impossible to exhaust this potential, I implored the Lord that He would continue to open the door ever wider, which He most definitely has!

What I have learned has gloriously changed my life, and done so in such a remarkable way as to defy description. The victory that I now have in Christ is that for which I had so long sought, and it is all because of the Cross. As well, the

Lord has opened up to me the joy of more abundant life (Jn. 10:10). In fact, every believer has more abundant life, but regrettably, most believers aren't enjoying it because they little understand its source.

GOLD

"And you shall overlay it with pure gold, and make thereto a crown of gold round about.

"And you shall make unto it a border of an hand breadth round about, and you shall make a golden crown to the border thereof round about" (Ex. 25:24-25).

The *"crown"* speaks of the kingly position of Christ, and with the crown covered in gold, along with the entirety of the table, it speaks of His deity.

The crown would tend to keep the bread in place so that it would not slip off the table, especially during times when Israel was instructed by the Lord to move. This speaks of the security of the believer, all in Christ.

It is interesting that the width of the crown is described as a *"hand breadth,"* which is approximately three to four inches high. All the dimensions of the Tabernacle otherwise are in cubits or half cubits.

This corresponds with the words of Christ, *"Neither shall any man pluck them out of My hand"* (Jn. 10:28).

There seems to have been a difference in the crown and the *"border."*

The border was, as well, to be the width of a hand and seems to have been a broad, flat bar placed about halfway down the legs, uniting them and holding them together. At the top of the bar, there was also to be a crown of gold.

THE RINGS AND THE STAVES

"And you shall make for it four rings of gold, and put the rings in the four corners that are on the four feet thereof.

"Over against the border shall the rings be for places of the staves to bear the table.

"And you shall make the staves of shittim wood, and overlay them with gold, that the table may be borne with them" (Ex. 25:26-28).

Wherever the Lord led Israel, even though it was in the wilderness, His Table accompanied them! So, wherever the Christian's lot may be cast, even though it may be in a prison, as with Paul, the believer can continue to feed on Christ, for Christ is ever with him.

It seems that the gold rings were placed at either end of the Table instead of the sides of the ark.

The staves for carrying the Table were made of indestructible wood and overlaid with gold. This again tells us of the humanity of Christ, i.e., the wood, and the gold, which typified His deity.

THE RINGS AND STAVES

THE DISHES

"And you shall make the dishes thereof, and spoons thereof, and covers thereof, and bowls thereof, to cover with all: of pure gold shall you make them" (Ex. 25:29).

The utensils and vessels were to be made of gold also.

The *"dishes"* were, no doubt, used by the priests when they ate the bread on the seventh day. The *"spoons"* and the *"covers"* were more than likely used in connection with the frankincense, which was to be poured over the bread, symbolizing the fragrance and purity of Christ.

The *"bowls"* were probably cups and were used in connection with the drink offerings, which were poured out before the Lord *"in the Holy Place"* (Num. 28:7). Pink said: *"The fact that the 'cups' used in connection with the 'drink offerings,' were placed upon the Table, tells us that Communion is the basis of thanksgiving!"*

PERPETUAL SHEWBREAD

"And you shall set upon the table shewbread before Me always" (Ex. 25:30).

As previously stated, the Covenant of the Cross is referred to as *"the blood of the Everlasting Covenant"* (Heb. 13:20). This means that the way has been Christ, even from the very beginning, the way presently is Christ, and the way will always be Christ, i.e., *"always."* More particularly, it is what Christ did, and I refer to the Cross.

Revelation, Chapters 21 and 22, proclaims the Perfect Age to come when Satan, fallen angels, and demons are forever locked away in the lake of fire. At that time, no more sin will be present in this world, and, in fact, the world and the universe will have been cleansed from all sin. At long last, the Son will have delivered the Kingdom up to the Father (I Cor. 15:24). Even then, Christ is referred to seven times in these last two chapters as *"the Lamb"* (Rev. 21:9, 14, 22, 23, 27; 22:1, 3). This appellative is used of Christ in order that we may know and realize that the glorious Perfect Age, which will most assuredly come and will last forever and forever, was, in fact, made possible by what Jesus did at the Cross. We are to never forget it, i.e., *"always."*

CHRIST, THE BREAD OF LIFE

"And you shall take fine flour, and bake twelve cakes thereof: two tenth deals shall be in one cake.

"And you shall set them in two rows, six on a row, upon the pure table before the Lord" (Lev. 24:5-6).

The *"fine flour,"* of which the cakes were made, speaks of flour that has been sifted minutely in order that all impurities be removed. It is a type of the perfect life of Christ. There was no coarseness or unevenness about Him. His life was perfect in every respect. In fact, it had to be this way in order that He keep the Law perfectly on our behalf, which He did.

We must ever understand that every single thing that He did was for us totally and completely, and not at all for Himself or for Heaven in any capacity. He, one might say, was our substitute. As the last Adam, He did what the first Adam did not do, which was to render a perfect obedience to God. The Scripture says: *"Then said I, Lo, I come (in the volume of the book it is written of Me,) to do Your will, O God"* (Heb. 10:7).

As each one of us looks at our lives, and no matter how consecrated we may be to the Lord, if we are honest, we will find much unevenness and coarseness in our personalities, in other words, things which aren't Christlike! However, Christ was perfect in His comportment, personality, demeanor, and, in fact, in every action. In word, thought, and deed, He left nothing to be desired.

TWELVE CAKES

The *"twelve cakes"* represented the Twelve Tribes of Israel, but, in reality, they represented much more.

The bread, as is obvious, was totally and completely a type of Christ, but the number of loaves being 12 represented His pure and perfect government. In fact, the entirety of the Law of Moses was, in reality, the government of God. It was that which the Lord required of the human race, inasmuch as it was His standard of righteousness. It was for the good of man everywhere, and totally for the good of man.

THE TWELVE CAKES

The biggest problem that Israel had was their circumventing the government of God, thereby, instituting their own government, which always and without exception brought ruin, as it always will bring ruin. That's the problem with the modern church and, in fact, always has been. Men tend to take that which is given by God, which is His perfect government, which is His Word, and then take from it or add to it. As this was the tragedy of Israel, it is likewise the tragedy of the church.

ACCORDING TO THE WORD OF GOD

As we've already stated several times in this volume, the criterion for all things must be, "Is it according to the Word of God?" If it's not according to the Word of God in every respect, then it's wrong and must be shunned and put away. However, men are fond of making rules, and especially religious men. They love to make rules, and they love to try to force others to obey those rules. In fact, the earth has been soaked with blood over religious wars more so than anything else. It is man attempting to have his religious way instead of God's way. Untold millions are in hell at this moment because they chose man's way, thereby, forsaking God's way. Listen to Solomon, *"There is a way which seems right unto a man, but the end thereof are the ways of death"* (Prov. 14:12).

Modern religious denominations are probably some of the worst offenders respecting this all-important subject. The constitution and bylaws of many denominations are made without any thought as to whether they are scriptural or not.

For instance, one major Pentecostal denomination changed its rulings the other day as it regards a particular subject. If what they had done previously was scriptural, how could they change it?

IS IT SCRIPTURAL?

The truth is, what they had done previously was not scriptural. I am persuaded that they have many more bylaws which aren't scriptural as well. Somehow, these men seem to think that because it's a denomination, which is, incidentally, man-instituted and man-directed, and they vote on certain things, all of this makes it right. It doesn't! It doesn't matter what man votes or says. Again we ask the question, *"Is it scriptural?"*

I was a member of a particular Pentecostal denomination for years, in fact, the very one I've just mentioned. While they have many godly preachers in that denomination, and while there are many godly people associated, as well, the truth is, their government is not scriptural, and as such, it does great harm to the work of God. Sadly, ultimately, this will destroy its effectiveness for the Lord. Regrettably, most other denominations fall into the same category.

God's government cannot be changed simply because it doesn't need to be changed. It was perfect when it was instituted, and it remains perfect.

FRANKINCENSE

"And you shall put pure frankincense upon each row, that it may be on the bread for a memorial, even an offering made by fire unto the LORD (Lev. 24:7).

The text seems to indicate that the frankincense was poured on the bread, but others who know the Hebrew claim that it really wasn't poured on the bread, but rather on the fire, hence, *"an offering made by fire unto the Lord."* Incidentally, the frankincense would have been burned on the Golden Altar, which was immediately in front of the Veil. Until the time of the burning, the frankincense would have been kept in two bowls, with each bowl sitting near or on each stack of six loaves.

The phrase, *"for a memorial,"* had to do with the following: As the frankincense would have been burned on the Golden Altar, it would have filled the Holy Place with a pungent aroma, signifying thankfulness to the Lord and that all blessings come from Him. Due to the fact that it was burned on the Golden Altar, it would have signified also the intercessory ministry of our Lord.

EVERY SABBATH

"Every Sabbath he shall set it in order before the LORD continually, being taken from the Children of Israel by an Everlasting Covenant.

"And it shall be Aaron's and his sons'; and they shall eat it in the Holy Place: for it is most holy unto him of the offerings of the LORD made by fire by a perpetual statute" (Lev. 24:8-9).

The *"Sabbath"* denoted *"rest,"* which, of course, pictured Christ. So, each Sabbath, the priests were to partake of this particular bread, thereby, symbolizing the partaking of Christ, with it replaced by 12 fresh loaves. The following is an account as to how it was done:

"Four priests entered the Holy Place, two of them carried on their hands the two stacks of the cakes, and two carried in their hands the two incense cups, four priests having gone in before them, two to take off the two old stacks, and

two to take off the two incense cups (frankincense). *Those who brought in the new stood at the north side with their faces to the south, and those who took away the old stood at the south side with their faces to the north.*

"As soon as the one party lifted up the old, the others put down the new, so that their hands were exactly over against each other, because it is written, 'Before My presence continually' (Ex. 25:30).

"The authorities during the second Temple took the expression 'continually' to denote that the cakes were not to be absent for one moment. Hence the simultaneous action of the two sets of priests, one lifting up the old, and the other at once putting down the new shewbread."

AN EVERLASTING COVENANT

The phrase, *"Being taken from the Children of Israel by an Everlasting Covenant,"* pertains to the fact that every person had to give one-half shekel of silver each year, which contributed annually toward the maintenance of the service in the Sanctuary, the securing of ingredients, etc.

"Silver" represented redemption, which is what Christ would bring about as a result of His death on the Cross. As it regards the division of the 12 cakes, it is said that the high priest took six, and the other priests had six, as well, among them. They were to eat the bread in the Holy Place. In fact, eight things were to be consumed within the precincts of the Sanctuary. They are as follows:

1. The remnant of the Meat Offering (Lev. 2:3, 10).
2. The flesh of the Sin Offering (Lev. 6:26).

3. The flesh of the Trespass Offering (Lev. 7:6).
4. The lepers' log of oil (Lev. 14:10).
5. The remainder of the omer (Lev. 23:10-11).
6. The Peace Offering of the congregation (Lev. 7:15).
7. The two loaves (Lev. 23:17-20).
8. The shewbread (Lev. 24:9).

THE SIXTH CHAPTER OF ST. JOHN

The things that Christ said, as recorded in Chapter 6 of John, portrays to us once again the true meaning of the shewbread. Actually, in Chapter 6 of John, Jesus very little explained the things that He said, rather taking the position that the massive crowd should have understood. In fact, they should have.

He said, *"Verily, verily, I say unto you, Moses gave you not that bread from Heaven; but My Father gives you the true bread from Heaven"* (Jn. 6:32).

In essence, Jesus was speaking of both the shewbread and the manna, but that bread was only a symbol. However, that which the Father would give would be *"the true bread from Heaven,"* namely the Lord Jesus Christ. Everything else preceding Him, no matter what it was, was only a symbol. He alone is the true bread. He then said, *"For the bread of God is He which comes down from Heaven, and gives life unto the world"* (Jn. 6:33).

This verse explains the plan of redemption for all of mankind.

The Bread of God, as stated, is Jesus Christ. The implication is that as physical bread is meant to be eaten and gives life to the physical body, likewise, Jesus, in the spiritual sense, must be experienced in the same manner.

When one accepts Christ as one's Saviour, the results are far more than the embracing of a philosophy, as it is with all other things. One literally becomes a part of the Body of Christ, with Him becoming a part of the believing sinner by virtue of imputed righteousness. Consequently, the statement, *"Bread of God,"* is meant to convey the impression that not only does the believer enter into life by the eating of this bread but, as well, sustains himself ever after in the same manner. It is such a *"oneness"* that Paul used the phrase, *"baptized into Jesus Christ"* (Rom. 6:3). Please understand, Paul was not speaking of water baptism, but rather the death of Christ on the Cross and us being in Him when He died, when He was buried, and when He was raised from the dead — all done by faith.

If we have been planted together in the likeness of His death (died with Him on the Cross, so to speak), understanding that, we are then raised with Him in the likeness of the new life, which helps us to live and have this resurrection life. However, it is all predicated on the Cross, *"planted in the likeness of His death."*

I AM THE BREAD OF LIFE

"And Jesus said unto them, I am the bread of life: he who comes to Me shall never hunger; and he who believes on Me shall never thirst" (Jn. 6:35).

The phrase, *"And Jesus said unto them, I am the bread of life,"* proclaims Him dropping all disguise and gathering up into one burning word all the previous teaching, which they might have fathomed but did not.

The Lord also referred to Himself, saying, *"I am the light of the world"* (Jn. 8:12). *"I am the good shepherd"* (Jn.

10:14), *"I am the resurrection and the life"* (Jn. 11:25), and, *"I am the true vine"* (Jn. 15:1).

The phrase, *"He who comes to Me shall never hunger,"* pertains to spiritual hunger.

There is a *"hunger"* in the heart of man, which cannot be satisfied by other things. Man was originally created in the image of God. As such, he is also a spiritual being and definitely not the product of mindless evolution; however, in his fallen state, he has cut himself off from God, who alone can satisfy this hunger.

If one is to notice, Jesus used the words, *"comes to Me,"* respecting the satisfaction of spiritual hunger, while He used the words, *"believes on Me,"* respecting the satisfying of spiritual thirst, for he had said, *"And he who believes on Me shall never thirst."* Consequently, these are the two requirements for salvation: one must *"come to Christ,"* and one must *"believe on Christ."*

Both hunger and thirst have to do with something that is perpetual, in other words, ongoing.

And yet, Jesus proclaims that upon receiving Him as one's Saviour, the spiritual hunger and thirst are forever ended, with never a recurrence.

I AM

Jesus says again, *"I am that bread of life"* (Jn. 6:48).

By using the words, *"I Am,"* Jesus plainly identifies Himself as the Jehovah of the Old Testament (Ex. 3:14).

Jesus was Jehovah, very God of very God, even then while He was very man. As man, He did not have the expression of deity, but He definitely had the possession of deity. In other words, He was just as much God in the Incarnation as He was when He dwelt *"in the light which no man can approach unto"* (I Tim. 6:16).

Jesus likened Himself as bread, and more perfectly, *"the bread of life."*

Why did Jesus use bread as a symbolism?

Bread is referred to in the natural as the *"staff of life,"* and that's exactly what it is.

So, as men eat natural bread to sustain the physical body, Jesus, as the spiritual bread, sustains the spiritual man, that is, if imbibed regularly.

The symbolism is intended to express the idea that as physical bread is to be eaten constantly, likewise, the believer is to feed on Jesus constantly.

THE CROSS

Jesus also said, *"I am the living bread which came down from Heaven: if any man eat of this bread, he shall live forever: and the bread that I will give is My flesh, which I will give for the life of the world"* (Jn. 6:51).

The phrase, *"And the bread that I will give is My flesh, which I will give for the life of the world,"* refers to the Cross. He was actually speaking there of the death that He would die and the manner in which He would die.

The Father prepared a perfect body for Him and did so that it might serve as a perfect sacrifice. However, for Him to serve as a perfect sacrifice, He would have to live the entirety of His life without sinning even one time in word, thought, or deed. He did that as our representative man, thereby, keeping the Law of God in every respect. As stated, He did it all for us. So, when the believing sinner accepts Christ upon simple faith in Christ and what He did for us at the Cross, such a person is instantly transferred from the position of *"lawbreaker"* to the position of *"lawkeeper."* This is true even though that believing sinner has broken the Law untold numbers of times, which merits death. It is all done by and through Christ.

You, the reader, must know and understand that the Cross of Christ is the foundation of the great plan of redemption. While everything else is, as stated, of utmost importance, still, it is the Cross which provides the means for all that we receive from God, and I mean all!

Then Jesus said words that literally hit like a thunderbolt over that vast crowd. He said, *"Verily, verily, I say unto you, Except you eat the flesh of the Son of Man, and drink His blood, you have no life in you"* (Jn. 6:53).

What did Jesus mean by such a statement?

He would say in just a few moments, *"It is the spirit who quickens; the flesh profits nothing: The words that I speak unto you, they are spirit, and they are life"* (Jn. 6:63).

In other words, He was saying that His statement was not meant to be taken literally.

So, exactly what did He mean by that shocking statement of eating His flesh and drinking His blood?

I will quote the text and the notes both from The Expositor's Study Bible.

The great apostle said, **"Do you not know, that so many of us as were baptized into Jesus Christ** (*plainly says that this baptism is into Christ and not water [I Cor. 1:17; 12:13; Gal. 3:27; Eph. 4:5; Col. 2:11-13]*) **were baptized into His death?** (*When Christ died on the Cross,* in the mind of God, we died with Him, in other words, He became our substitute, and our identification with Him in His death gives us all the benefits for which He died; the idea is that He did it all for us!)

"**Therefore we are buried with Him by baptism into death** (not only did we die with Him, but we were buried with Him as well, which means that all the sin and transgression of the past were buried; when they put Him in the tomb, they put all of our sins into that tomb as well!): **that like as Christ was raised up from the dead by the glory of the Father, even so we also should walk in newness of life** (we died with Him, we were buried with Him, and His resurrection was our resurrection to a 'newness of life').

"**For if we have been planted together** (with Christ) **in the likeness of His death** (Paul proclaims the Cross as the instrument through which all blessings come; consequently, the Cross must ever be the object of our faith, which gives the Holy Spirit latitude to work within our lives), **we shall be also in the likeness of His resurrection.** (We can have the likeness of His resurrection, only as long as we understand the 'likeness of His death,' which refers to the Cross as the means by which all of this is done)" **(Rom. 6:3-5).**

As previously stated, this is the way that we are given life in our born-again experience, and it's also the way in which we live this life and have victory over the world, the flesh, and the Devil.

So, when Jesus addressed the great crowd, which is recorded in Chapter 6 of John, He was showing them the true bread which came from Heaven, namely Himself, and, in effect, constituted the fulfillment of the *"Table of Shew-*

bread," and, as well, *"the manna."* That bread, which only served as a symbol, ultimately perished, but Jesus Christ, in the life that He gives and we receive, is all done by faith. However, it must be faith in Christ and what He did for us at the Cross. Then we have the true Bread of Life, and we will never hunger again, even as we will never thirst again. Only then can the craving in the human heart be satisfied, for God alone can satisfy such, simply because He is our Creator, and we were created in His image.

"Drawn to the Cross which You have blessed,
"With healing gifts for soul's distress,
"To find in You my life, my rest,
"Christ crucified, I come."

"Stained with the sins which I have wrought,
"In word and deed and secret thought,
"For pardon which Your blood has bought,
"Christ crucified, I come."

"Weary of selfishness and pride,
"False pleasures gone, vain hopes denied,
"Deep in Your wounds my shame to hide,
"Christ crucified, I come."

"You know all my griefs and fears,
"Your grace abused, my misspent years;
"Yet now to You for cleansing tears,
"Christ crucified I come."

"I would not, if I could conceal
"The ills which only You canst heal;
"So to the Cross where sinners kneel,
"Christ crucified, I come."

"Wash me, and take away each stain,
"Let nothing of my sin remain;
"For cleansing, though it be through pain,
"Christ crucified, I come."

"And then for work to do for Thee,
"Which shall so sweet a service be,
"That angels well might envy me,
"Christ crucified, I come."

"A life of labour, prayers, and love
"Which shall my heart's conversion prove,
"Till to a glorious rest above,
"Christ crucified, I come."

"To share with You Your life divine,
"Your righteousness, Your likeness mine,
"Since You have made my nature Thine,
"Christ crucified, I come."

"To be what You would have me be,
"Accepted, sanctified in Thee,
"Through what Your grace shall work in me,
"Christ crucified, I come."

8

The Altar of Incense

CHAPTER EIGHT

The Altar of Incense

"AND YOU SHALL make an altar to burn incense upon: Of shittim wood shall you make it.

"A cubit shall be the length thereof, and a cubit the breadth thereof: foursquare shall it be: and two cubits shall be the height thereof: the horns thereof shall be of the same.

"And you shall overlay it with pure gold, the top thereof, and the sides thereof round about, and the horns thereof; and you shall make unto it a crown of gold round about" (Ex. 30:1-3).

Back in Exodus, Chapter 25, instructions were given to Moses as it regarded the Ark of the Covenant, the Table of Shewbread, and the Golden Lampstand. The latter two were in the Holy Place, and the Ark of the Covenant was in the Holy of Holies. It has been conjectured as to why the Holy Spirit didn't give the dimensions for the Altar of Incense when the instructions were given regarding the Table and the Lampstand.

As well, instructions for the Brazen Altar were given in Exodus, Chapter 27, but no mention was made there of the Brazen Laver, which was the second vessel outside of the Tabernacle, actually, the one which sat immediately in front of the door. It instead is detailed in Chapter 30 of Exodus, along with the Altar of Incense.

THE HOLY SPIRIT

We know that every single word in the Bible was given by the Holy Spirit, and, of course, we speak of the original text. We know, as well, that the order of material given in each book was superintended by the Holy Spirit also. All of this means that it is error free. Now, when we use the term *"error free,"* we are not speaking of the translation or of the chapter and verse divisions. Those things were done by men and are subject to mistakes, but we do claim the original text to be perfect.

Unfortunately, there aren't any original texts left, but there are thousands of copies of those texts, some reaching back to the year 300 A.D. Scholarship says that if there are as many as 10 copies of any proven work, it is looked at as authentic. The truth is, there are more copies of the Scriptures, both Old and New Testaments, than any other work in existence, a thousand times over. Actually, there are more than 10,000 copies of books of the Bible, or portions thereof, so the authenticity of the original text is not in doubt. I have read behind quite a number of authors as it concerns the chronological order of that of which we speak. To be frank, there are about as many reasons given for the manner in which the Holy Spirit presented the text as there are writers. We do know that the Holy Spirit saved the instructions for these two vessels for this particular chapter, but no one really knows why. Any suggestion is speculation at best; considering that, I will remain silent as it regards this particular question.

INCENSE

The Golden Altar was designed by the Lord for the purpose of burning incense. In the latter part of Chapter 30 of Exodus, the various spices are given that make up the incense, to which we will address ourselves at that time.

The purpose and reason for this incense was to symbolize the intercession made by our Lord since the Cross on a continuing basis for all believers and for all time. The Cross is what made the intercessory work of our Lord possible. Paul said, *"He* (Christ) *ever lives to make intercession for them"* (Heb. 7:25).

Just how does Christ make intercession for all the saints, of which the Golden Altar was a type?

Sometime back, I was reading behind one of the great theologians, who is now with the Lord. He was stating that Christ prays for us before the throne of God, etc. In other words, this was the manner of His intercession.

That is incorrect, and it is incorrect simply because the necessity of doing such would mean that the work carried out at the Cross was unfinished.

THE WORK AT THE CROSS WAS COMPLETE

To properly understand the intercession of Christ, we must first understand that His work at the Cross was total and complete. It was a finished work, and that term means exactly what it says. When Jesus said, *"It is finished,"* this meant that the price had been fully and totally paid for the redemption of humanity, at least for those who will believe (Jn. 19:30; 3:16).

Even though we have a perfect redemption, we, as the receptacles of this perfect redemption, aren't perfect within ourselves. In fact, all believers still have a *"sin nature"* (Rom. 6:1-2, 6-7, 10-13, etc.).

In every Scripture we've given where the word *"sin"* is used, in the original text, it had in front of that particular word what is referred to as *"the definite article."* In other words, it said *"the* sin," which refers to the sin nature.

I realize that many preachers claim that believers no longer have a sin nature. If that is the case, then the Holy Spirit wasted a lot of time explaining to us through Paul how to have victory over this malady of darkness. Victory is achieved by the believer, even as we've already stated enumerable times, by understanding that all comes through the Cross, which must ever be the object of our faith. Understanding that we definitely do have a sin nature, the truth is, all believers still fail the Lord at times. The Bible doesn't teach sinless perfection, but it does teach that sin is not to have dominion over us (Rom. 6:14).

JESUS CHRIST IS OUR GREAT HIGH PRIEST

As it regards sin on the part of the Christian, John told us to *"sin not,"* but then he said, *"If any man sin, we have an advocate with the Father, Jesus Christ the Righteous:*

"And He is the propitiation for our sins: and not for ours only, but also for the sins of the whole world" (I Jn. 2:1-2).

Christ is our advocate and our mediator. As such, He is our high priest. Paul said of Him, *"We have such an high priest, who is set on the right hand of the throne of the Majesty in the heavens"* (Heb. 8:1). This high priest is *"Holy, harmless, undefiled, separate from sinners, and made higher than the heavens"* (Heb. 7:26).

Understanding that as our high priest, He intercedes for us, exactly how does He do such?

Paul also said, *"For Christ is not entered into the holy places made with hands, which are the figures of the true; but into Heaven itself, now to appear in the presence of God for us"* (Heb. 9:24).

In Verse 24, we are told how He makes intercession for us. *"Now to appear in the presence of God for us,"* tells us that His appearance in the presence of God, which refers to the throne of God, guarantees our intercession. He doesn't really have to do anything, and, in fact, He doesn't do anything. He doesn't have to pray, He doesn't have to ask, and He has to perform no work. His appearance proclaims the fact that He has paid the price and that God has fully accepted that price, which guarantees intercession by Christ for all the saints for all time. That's the way that His intercession works. His work at the Cross was a finished work, meaning that it left nothing to be further done. All was accomplished at the Cross, with nothing left hanging, so to speak. Let me say it again: if Christ had to pray physically for us before the Father whenever we needed something, that would mean that what He did at the Cross was not complete and had to have something added. We know that is basely incorrect. Paul said: **"Wherefore He** (*The Lord Jesus Christ*) **is able also to save them to the uttermost** (*proclaims the fact that Christ alone has made the only true atonement for sin; He did this at the Cross*) **who come unto God by Him** (*proclaims the only manner in which man can come to God*)**, seeing He ever lives to make interces-**

sion for them" (*His very presence by the right hand of the Father guarantees such, with nothing else having to be done*) **(Heb. 1:3).**

"For such an high priest became us (*presents the fact that no one less exalted could have met the necessities of the human race*)**, Who is holy, harmless, undefiled, separate from sinners** (*describes the spotless, pure, perfect character of the Son of God as our Great High Priest; as well, this tells us that Christ did not become a sinner on the Cross, as some claim, but was rather the Sin Offering*)**, and made higher than the heavens"** (*Refers to the fact that He is seated at the right hand of the Father, which is the most exalted position in Heaven, or earth*) **(Heb. 7:25-26).**

THE SIZE OF THE ALTAR

This altar was 18 inches long and 18 inches wide. It was three feet high. As is obvious, it was foursquare. In its application to Christ Himself, this tells us that His intercession embraces all His people.

The altar was made of *"shittim wood,"* i.e., *"indestructible wood,"* which, as we've already stated, portrayed the humanity of Christ in all its perfection.

This indestructible wood was overlaid with pure gold, which typified His deity. This is the God-Man, Jesus Christ!

The altar had four horns protruding outward from all corners, once again portraying power. Our dominion is in Christ and Christ alone! However, the dominion of which we speak, and which the altar represented, is a total dominion, hence, the horns on all four corners. This means that the believer should be victorious in every capacity of his or her life. What Jesus did at the Cross was complete, and that means a complete victory, which was all done for you and me.

We can have that complete victory if we look exclusively to Him, ever making the Cross the object of our faith. That being the case, the Holy Spirit guarantees the victory (Rom. 8:11).

There was a *"crown of gold"* all the way around the altar, which signified the kingly character of Christ.

THE STAVES

"And two golden rings shall you make to it under the crown of it, by the two corners thereof, upon the two sides of it shall you make it; they shall be for places for the staves to bear it withal.

"And you shall make the staves of shittim wood, and overlay them with gold" (Ex. 30:4-5).

There were to be two golden rings on the altar, one on either side, through which staves could be placed in order for the altar to be carried when the camp was moved.

"Two" is the number of *"witness"* and speaks of the Holy Spirit, who is here to testify of Christ (Jn. 15:26). The *"staves"* of wood, overlaid with gold, intimate that it is the God-Man whom the Spirit is here to glorify.

These rings and staves are, as well, a proclamation of our pilgrim character, in other words, that this world is not our home but that we are merely traveling through.

THE POSITION OF THE ARK

"And you shall put it before the Veil that is by the Ark of the Testimony, before the Mercy Seat that is over the Testimony where I will meet with you" (Ex. 30:6).

The Golden Ark was positioned in the Holy Place immediately in front of the beautiful Veil, which hid the Holy of Holies, which contained the Ark of the Covenant. Consequently, only the Veil separated the Altar of Incense from the Ark of the Covenant, which meant they were only a very few feet apart.

Even though the Veil separated these two sacred vessels, the very fact that they were this close tells us that the separation was only temporary. Upon the Cross being a fact, the veil, spiritually speaking, was removed, and now Christ our intercessor is in the very presence of God, all on our behalf. In a sense of the word, and presently speaking, the Altar of Incense, signifying intercession and worship, has now become one with the Ark of the Covenant, signifying the throne of God (Heb. 1:3; 9:24).

(The Ark of the Testimony is the Ark of the Covenant, and the Testimony is the Ten Commandments).

THE INCENSE

"And the LORD said unto Moses, Take unto you sweet spices, stacte, and onycha, and galbanum: these sweet spices with pure frankincense: of each shall there be a like weight" (Ex. 30:34).

These were the spices, properly mixed together, which made the incense that was to be poured over the coals of fire on the Altar of Incense, brought from the Brazen Altar. This was to be done twice a day, which would fill the Holy Place with a smoke of sorts, which had a very pleasant aroma. It was meant to typify the intercession of our Lord after His work was complete on the Cross, and He had appeared in the presence of God, all on our behalf. This has now been done and is being done. In other words, His intercession continues unto this hour and will ever continue.

The particular spices were meant to typify His work as it regards intercession. However, all of it was tied to the Cross, hence, the coals of fire from the Brazen Altar, the altar which typified His crucifixion.

Without going into detail as it regards the origin of these particular spices, suffice to say, they each typified Christ and were, as the spices for the holy anointing oil, produced as a result of cutting, crushing, or both.

It seems that of each of these spices, they were all to be used in the same amount.

A PERFUME

"And you shall make it a perfume, a confection after the art of the apothecary, tempered together, pure and holy" (Ex. 30:35).

Pulpit said, *"Like the holy oil, the incense was to be artistically compounded by one accustomed to deal with such ingredients."*

As is surely noticed, the directions for all of this were explicit. All of it represented Christ, and so nothing was to be done after human ingenuity.

The concoction was to be a *"perfume,"* which referred to the fact that the smoke from the incense would have a very pleasant aroma and would fill the Holy Place, typical of the intercession of Christ before the Father, once again, all on our behalf. The very word *"perfume"* presents the fact that God the Son will always represent us in a very positive manner, as, of course, should be obvious. Irrespective of our conduct on earth, that which comes to the Father as it regards the Son is always of a very pleasant aroma, one might say!

BEFORE THE TESTIMONY

"And you shall beat some of it very small, and put of it before the Testimony in the Tabernacle of the congregation, where I will meet with you: it shall be unto you most holy" (Ex. 30:36).

The idea seems to be that some was to be kept before the Altar of Incense constantly, so a supply would ever be available. As well, it presents the fact that Christ *"ever lives to make intercession for us"* (Heb. 7:25).

Considering that the incense was very near the vicinity of the divine presence, it rendered it *"most holy."*

Again we emphasize that our conduct may not at all times be *"most holy,"* but to be sure, His intercession for us is always *"most holy."*

THE SENTENCE OF DEATH

"And as for the perfume which you shall make, you shall not make to yourselves according to the composition thereof: it shall be under you wholly for the LORD.

"Whosoever shall make like unto that, the smell thereto, shall be cut off from his people" (Ex. 30:37-38).

If this *"perfume"* was ever used to be placed on the physical bodies of individuals, these persons were to be executed by civil authorities. It was *"most holy"* and was to be used exclusively for its designed purpose.

Before the Cross, it is not certain as to exactly how much the priests knew as it regarded the antitype. It is easy for us to look back now and discern, at least to a point, the meaning of these *"types."* However, before the fact, it would not have been so simple. They were given the Word of the Lord, that it was most holy, and that it was never to be used other than for that which it had been designed. To ignore this command, to be sure, would insure the judgment of God.

THE BURNING OF INCENSE

"And Aaron shall burn thereon sweet incense every morning: when he dresses the lamps, he shall burn incense upon it.

"And when Aaron lights the lamps at evening, he shall burn incense upon it, a perpetual incense before the Lord throughout your generations" (Ex. 30:7-8).

The incense was to be burned morning and evening, perhaps at about the time that the sacrifices were offered, which would have been 9 a.m. and 3 p.m. It was burned in the following manner: the priest who was officiating would take one or more coals of fire from the Brazen Altar, place them on top of the Golden Altar, and then pour incense over the coals, with the resultant cloud and fragrance filling the Holy Place. As stated, it represented the intercession of the Lord Jesus Christ, our Great High Priest, on behalf of the saints. Of course, this was only a symbol and was actually a symbol in two ways:

1. Jesus had not yet gone to the Cross; therefore, the representation was future.
2. As would be obvious, this which the priests did twice a day was only symbolic. Also, we might quickly add

that the intercession of Christ presently includes the making of our worship acceptable unto the Lord.

If it is to be noticed, before this worship could commence, the sacrifices had to be offered. This meant in symbolic form that His precious blood had first to be poured out before the Spirit could be poured forth; and sinners must first be washed from their sins in that precious blood before they can receive the Holy Spirit. Thus, cleansed and sanctified, worship at the Golden Altar of Incense is possible, but not otherwise.

THE INGREDIENTS OF INCENSE

- Stacte: some identify this incense with the gum of the storay tree.
- Onycha: from shellfish found in the Red Sea.
- Galbanum: it is a resinous gum of brownish-yellow color; the plant which yields this gum has not been determined.
- Frankincense: a bitter white substance that came from piercing a tree that grew in the cracks of marble rock.

PERPETUAL

Concerning this, Williams said: *"God having brought His people out of Egypt, established the Brazen Altar outside the Tabernacle, and the Golden Altar inside; and appointed a mediator to maintain relationship with Him* (the high priest) *in order that He might dwell among them. The Brazen Altar symbolized the perfection of Christ's sacrifice for sin; the Golden Altar, the preciousness of His person. The Altar itself spoke of Jesus, and what He would do on the Cross to redeem humanity. The wood and the gold prefigured His humanity and deity; it was crowned, and it had staves to bear it so as to be the day and night companion of a pilgrim people. The incense burned upon it spoke of Him. Aaron himself, in his robes of glory, pictured Him; and the light of the Golden Lampstand foretold Him, who being the light of that world that needs no sun came into this world to be its light."*

Williams went on to say: *"The fire of Verse 7, and the blood of Verse 10, teach that there can be no acceptable worship apart from atonement."*

The word *"perpetual"* in Verse 8 doesn't mean for eternity, but rather as long as the first covenant lasted. When Jesus came, He, being the incense, fulfilled the symbol, with there being no more need for such presently because Christ is now in Heaven, appearing in the presence of God on our behalf (Heb. 9:24). Of course, I speak of the New Covenant.

STRANGE INCENSE

"You shall offer no strange incense thereon, nor burnt sacrifice, nor meat offering; neither shall you pour drink offering thereon" (Ex. 30:9).

We know from Leviticus 16:12-13 and Numbers 16:46 that the coals of fire placed on the Golden Altar were taken from off of the Brazen Altar, where the sin offering was consumed. There was, therefore, a very intimate connection between the two altars: the activities of the latter were based squarely upon those of the former; in other words, the incense was kindled upon that fire, which had first fed upon the sacrifice, thus, identifying the priests' service at both altars.

Concerning this, Pink said: *"This, in figure, tells us that our Great High Priest expects no blessings which His blood has not purchased, and expects pardon from divine justice for no sins for which faith has not been evidenced. And incidentally, the measure of the blessings which are given is God's estimate of the life which He gave. In His mediatorial prayer in John, Chapter 17, before He presents a single petition concerning His people, Christ said, 'I have glorified You on the earth; I have finished the work which You gave Me to do' (Jn. 17:4). That was the foundation on which all His pleas were based and urged."*

So, it is imperative that three things be done here.

THREE THINGS

1. The coals of fire had to come from the Brazen Altar, which represented the Cross of Calvary. This tells us, as stated, that all intercession and all worship, at least that which is recognized by the Lord, is based squarely on what Jesus did at the Cross. If any other type of fire would be used on that Golden Altar, the priests would be stricken dead just as, in fact, Nadab and Abihu actually were (Lev. 10:1-2).

Unfortunately, untold thousands of churches have abandoned the Cross and are, in fact, offering *"strange fire."* Spiritual death is the result!

2. The coals of fire had to be placed on the Golden Altar, which refers to a faith and dependence placed in Christ as it regards His intercession, all on our behalf. Let it quickly be stated, such cannot be done, and, in

fact, such will not be done until there is faith in what the Brazen Altar represents. As stated, the two — the Brazen Altar with its finished work and the Golden Altar and its intercessory work — go hand in hand.

3. The incense poured on the burning coals had to be that which the Lord had designed and no other kind. Anything else would be called *"strange incense"* and would be unacceptable! We must understand that this incense pictured and portrayed Christ in His atoning work. That and that alone is what God will recognize. Once again, we speak exclusively of the Cross! Everything is based on the Cross! Everything stems from the Cross!

THE BLOOD

"And Aaron shall make an atonement upon the horns of it once in a year with the blood of the sin offering of atonements: once in the year shall he make atonement upon it throughout your generations: it is most holy unto the LORD" (Ex. 30:10).

This particular verse speaks of the Great Day of Atonement, which took place once a year. On that day, the high priest would sacrifice a clean animal, remove his garments of glory and beauty, and take the blood of that slain victim into the Holy of Holies, where it would be applied to the Mercy Seat on the Ark of the Covenant. Actually, he would do this three times. The first time was to fill the Holy of Holies with incense. Secondly, it would be for himself in that he was a sinful man, despite the fact that he was the high priest. Then, most of all, it was for the sins of the nation of Israel. Always, their salvation, as well as our salvation, was based and is based on blood atonement.

As well, he would apply some of that blood on the horns of the Golden Altar. So, in essence, we have two factors at work here:

1. The blood applied to the Mercy Seat speaks of our salvation, in other words, what makes the born-again experience possible!

2. The blood applied to the horns of the Golden Altar at that particular time spoke of our sanctification. To which we've already eluded, horns in the Bible represent dominion. The very fact that these horns were on the Golden Altar tells us that the Lord expects us to have dominion over every single sin, barring none! As well, this can be done only by one's faith in Christ and what Christ did for us at the Cross, symbolized by the blood.

SACRIFICES AND THE ALTAR OF INCENSE

All of this which we've just said concerning the blood applied to the horns once a year harks back to Verse 9. The Lord through Moses informed the priests that no *"burnt sacrifice, or meat offering, or drink offering,"* was to be used on the Altar of Incense.

Why?

Sin in its totality is handled at the Brazen Altar, i.e., the Cross. The Altar of Incense, which speaks of intercession and worship, is not meant to atone for sin. So, when the believer thinks that he can overcome sin by increasing his prayer life, by fasting more, by witnessing to souls, by giving more money, or by experiencing manifestations of any kind, he will never find victory in that manner. While all of these things may be good in their own right, he will find that his faith is wrong, and His faith regarding overcoming strength must ever rest in the Cross of Christ. That alone will guarantee victory. However, this is a lesson that the modern church seems not to have learned. It keeps trying to gain victory in all the wrong ways. Because it's so important, let's say it again: all victory is found at the Cross and the Cross alone! The coals of fire taken from the Brazen Altar to the Altar of Incense speaks of a work already done and completed. For us to add to that, we are, in essence, saying that what was done at the Brazen Altar was not enough, in effect, that the sacrifice was not enough. As should be obvious, God can never honor such. This comes back to what Paul said: *"That if you be circumcised, Christ shall profit you nothing"* (Gal. 5:2).

It's not what one does, but rather what one believes, and if one believes right, then one will do right.

"My heart was not right,
"In my dear Saviour's sight,
"I knew not the peace all sublime;
"I came to His side,
"And His blood was applied,
"Hallelujah, I know He is mine!"

"My soul was distressed,
"With its sorrow oppressed,
"Till Jesus my Saviour I found,
"But now He's my theme,
"While His Word keeps me clean;
"Hallelujah, His grace does abound!"

"I walk in the light,
"Of His presence so bright,
"His love makes my heaven below,
"I'll sing of His grace,
"Till I see His dear face,
"With the dear ones washed whiter than snow."

9

The Golden Candlestick

CHAPTER NINE

The Golden Candlestick

"AND YOU SHALL make a candlestick of pure gold: of beaten work shall the candlestick be made: his shaft, and his branches, his bowls, his knops, and his flowers, shall be of the same" (Ex. 25:31).

The Lampstand, unlike many of the other vessels, was made of pure gold. It contained no indestructible wood, which served as a type of the humanity of Christ, and yet, the next phrase does, in a sense, speak of His humanity.

Incidentally, the Hebrew word *"M'nourah"* means *"lightbearer"* and should have been translated *"lampstand"* instead of *"candlestick."* A candlestick holds candles, and there were no candles on this particular sacred vessel.

If you had come through the front door of the Tabernacle, the Lampstand would have sat to your left, which would have been the south side, for the Tabernacle always faced the east.

None but priests could enter the Holy Place, so, in essence, the people of Israel did not actually ever see the Golden Lampstand.

THE ONLY SOURCE OF LIGHT

The Lampstand was the only source of light in the entirety of the Holy Place; consequently, the priests could see to eat the shewbread and offer up incense on the Golden Altar only by the light of the Lampstand.

The Lampstand is a type of Christ as the light of the world, whether in His earthly ministry, pertaining to His first advent, or through His church. While believers are the light of the world presently, we are such light only as a reflection of Christ (Mat. 5:14).

The Lampstand, as well, portrays the Holy Spirit, typified by the oil, in His work within and upon Christ (Lk. 4:18-19).

OF BEATEN WORK

The phrase, *"Of beaten work shall the lampstand be made,"* portrays the second time the word *"beaten"* is used, the first being the Cherubim (Ex. 25:18).

In the literal sense, the word *"beaten"* refers to the fact that the Lampstand was not cast in a mold, but was rather fashioned by hand. This means the entire Lampstand was fashioned and made out of one piece of gold, which some say no craftsman in the world presently could do such a thing.

In the spiritual sense, it refers to the humanity of Christ, God becoming man, which, in actuality, is beyond our comprehension. The Creator becoming a creature is beyond our pale of understanding, but that's what happened!

Normally, as it regards the Tabernacle, gold typifies the deity of Christ, with wood typifying His humanity; however, here it is different simply because there was no wood. This we must understand: His humanity was perfect, in effect, just as perfect as had been and was His deity. He was not born in sin as are all other human beings, but was born of the Virgin Mary. In other words, His conception had nothing to do with the seed of Joseph or the egg of Mary. She only supplied a habitation for His nine months of development.

Jesus was absolutely without sin in every capacity. That means in His life and living, He never sinned even one time, whether by word, thought, or deed. No other human being could say such a thing. And yet, when we accept Him as our Saviour, He freely awards us His perfection. So, when we see the middle stem of the Lampstand, we are seeing Christ, but more so, we are seeing the perfection of Christ.

THE SUFFERING OF CHRIST

"Beaten" speaks of the suffering of Christ, and by that, we refer to the Cross. He is now glorified and is done so as the reward of His perfect but painful work.

Due to His finished work, Christ now occupies an even greater position than before His Incarnation. The Scripture says of Him, *"And being found in fashion as a man, He humbled Himself and became obedient unto death, even the death of the Cross.*

"Wherefore God also has highly exalted Him, and given Him a name which is above every name" (Phil. 2:8-9).

Considering that Christ is God and that He has always been perfect, how can perfection become greater?

In fact, perfection cannot be made greater; however, one can definitely add to perfection, and this is exactly what happened with Christ.

He is Creator, but due to His atoning work on the Cross of Calvary, He is also now Saviour, which makes Him more exalted than ever before (Heb. 1:3-4).

THE BOWLS, THE KNOPS, AND THE FLOWERS

The three items of the heading could be translated *"cups, pomegranates, and lilies."*

The *"bowls"* or *"cups"* form the first ornament on each branch and are likened to almonds, which signify the Resurrection (Num. 17:1-8).

The *"knops"* could have been translated *"pomegranates,"* which speak of fruit.

The *"flowers"* could have been translated *"lilies"* and speak of purity. The lily blossoms supported the lamps, which were separate.

So, the Lampstand, in its portrayal of light, speaks of resurrection, which pertains to the believing sinner being baptized into the death of Christ, buried with Him by baptism into death, and then raised with Him in *"newness of life,"* which speaks of resurrection, i.e., "resurrection life" (Rom. 6:5).

This particular passage doesn't speak of the coming resurrection, but rather the resurrection of a new life as it regards the born-again experience. However, as it concerns this, Paul said, *"If we have been planted in the likeness of His death, we shall be also in the likeness of His resurrection"* (Rom. 6:5). In other words, before we can properly live and have this resurrection life in Christ on a daily basis — living the resurrection life which is intended by the Lord — we must understand that this is afforded because of the Cross, and only because of the Cross.

FRUIT

As Christ now lives through the believer and, thereby, is aided by the Holy Spirit, even as the believer maintains his faith in the finished work of Christ, he now begins to bring forth fruit.

Jesus said, *"I am the vine, you are the branches: he who abides in Me, and I in him* (Rom. 6:3-5; Jn. 14:20), *the same brings forth much fruit: for without Me you can do nothing"* (Jn. 15:5).

The *"lily"* speaks of purity, which one can have only as one looks totally to Christ and what Christ has done at the Cross. The individual cannot make himself pure, that being a work entirely of the Holy Spirit. He functions entirely upon the basis of the finished work of Christ, thereby, demanding that we always have and maintain faith in that great sacrifice.

BRANCHES

"And six branches shall come out of the sides of it; three branches of the lampstand out of the one side, and three branches of the lampstand out of the other side" (Ex. 25:32).

There is tremendous spiritual meaning in the design of the Lampstand. It had three branches to the side, totaling six, which is the number of man, and which is the Body of Christ, whether Israel or the church. Actually, in Christ, we have been *"made both one"* (Eph. 2:14).

Verse 36 tells us that the entirety of the Lampstand was *"one beaten work of pure gold,"* meaning that these branches were not welded or fastened to the side of the main stem, but were rather a part of the main stem. This speaks of our being *"in Christ."*

THE BRANCHES

Paul used the term *"in Christ,"* or one of its derivatives, such as *"in Him,"* some 170 times in his 14 epistles. We are in Christ, as stated, by virtue of being baptized into His death, buried with Him by baptism into death, and then raised with Him in newness of life (Rom. 6:3-4). As well, it should be understood that whenever Paul used the word *"baptism"* here, he wasn't speaking of water baptism, but rather being baptized into Christ, which comes by faith, and which takes place when we are born again.

This tells us how significant the Cross is to the believer. It is the manner by which we were able to be grafted into Christ. This makes us *"one with Christ,"* which, in effect, is intended. Without proper faith in the Cross, there is no union with Christ, as should be obvious!

THE APPEARANCE OF THE BRANCHES

"Three bowls made like unto almonds, with a knop and a flower in one branch; and three bowls made like almonds in the other branch, with a knop and a flower: so in the six branches that come out of the candlestick" (Ex. 25:33).

The ornamentation of these branches seems to be as follows: there were three *"bowls"* shaped like almond blossoms, with each branch having the same number. The three were then followed by a pomegranate and a lily flower.

We might ask the question as to why there were three bowls (almond blossoms) on each stem and only one pomegranate and only one lily.

This tells us that the almond blossom, which represents resurrection, which speaks of the Cross, is the foundation on which everything is based. This is where the emphasis must always be. This is why Paul said, *"For Christ sent me not to baptize, but to preach the Gospel: not with wisdom of words, lest the Cross of Christ should be made of none effect"* (I Cor. 1:17).

As well, we must ever understand that we have resurrection life only as we understand the Crucifixion and what it means to us. We have already dealt with this once, but because it is so very, very important, please allow the repetition. Paul said, *"For if we have been planted together in the likeness of His death, we shall be also in the likeness of His resurrection"* (Rom. 6:5).

Many Christians are fond of saying that they are *"resurrection people."* That is true only if we understand that *"we have been planted together in the likeness of His death,"* which, of course, speaks of the Cross. The victory was won at the Cross, with the Resurrection being one of the results and benefits of that victory. In fact, if Jesus had failed to atone for even one sin, even a small sin, due to the fact that *"the wages of sin is death,"* He could not have been raised from the dead. So, we understand from that that all the victory, and I mean all, was won totally and completely at the Cross.

Paul said as well, *"But God forbid that I should glory, save in the Cross of our Lord Jesus Christ, by whom the world is crucified unto me, and I unto the world"* (Gal. 6:14).

I remind the reader that Paul didn't say, *"But God forbid that I should glory, save in the resurrection of our Lord Jesus Christ ...."*

Of course, Paul, in fact, did glory in the Resurrection as any true believer will; however, he said what he said simply because the victory is in the Cross, and I mean all the victory. Whenever Jesus said, *"It is finished, into Your hands I commend My Spirit,"* at that moment, the veil in the Temple rent from top to bottom, showing that the price had been paid and accepted by the Father and redemption was complete.

To be frank, the Resurrection was never in doubt. Jesus knew that what He set out to do — atone for all sin, past, present, and future — would be accomplished, and it was. That being done, there was nothing that could keep Him from being raised from the dead.

If we properly understand the Cross, we will have resurrection life, and the *"fruit of the Spirit,"* typified by the pomegranates, will be developed in our lives, which will always result in purity, represented by the lily, i.e., flower.

THE CENTRAL SHAFT

"And in the lampstand shall be four bowls made like unto almonds, with their knops and their flowers" (Ex. 25:34).

By the short phrase, *"And in the lampstand,"* we know that Moses is speaking of the central shaft or stem. Where the branches had three bowls with one knop and one flower, the middle stem had four bowls, along with four knops and four flowers. This made 12 ornaments, which spoke of the government of Christ.

This tells us that His government has the Cross as its foundation, which will produce much fruit and much purity. There were five ornaments on each stem, three bowls with one knop and one flower. Five is the number of grace and means that we as believers have these great qualities not at all because of our merit, but strictly because of the grace of God (Eph. 2:8-9).

While there are many definitions of the term *"grace,"* still, the idea is, grace is simply the goodness of God extended to undeserving people.

THE BRANCHES

"And there shall be a knop under two branches of the same, and a knop under two branches of the same, and a knop under two branches of the same, according to the six branches that proceed out of the lampstand.

"Their knops and their branches shall be of the same: all it shall be one beaten work of pure gold" (Ex. 25:35-36).

Two things are said here:

1. Addressing the latter first, even as we've already stated, the entirety of the Lampstand was of one piece of gold, crafted according to the design given by the Holy Spirit, and exactly according to the design given by the Holy Spirit.
2. Even though the branches came out even at the top, even with the main shaft, as would be obvious, the outward branch would be the longest of all, with the middle branch next to the longest, with the branch closest to the stem being the shortest. But yet, all of them had the same number of ornamentation.

This tells us that all believers can enjoy resurrection life, bear fruit, and develop purity. Of course, all of this is a work of the Holy Spirit, which we shall see.

THE SEVEN LAMPS

"And you shall make the seven lamps thereof: and they shall light the lamps thereof, that they may give light over against it.

"And the tongs thereof, and the snuffdishes thereof, shall be of pure gold.

"Of a talent of pure gold shall he make it, with all these vessels.

"And look that you make them after their pattern, which was showed you in the mount" (Ex. 25:37-40).

- The *"lamps"* were at the top of each branch in the main stem. They were separate from the ornamentation.

- There were *"seven"* of these lamps, which speaks of perfect illumination, which only the Holy Spirit can do. If we follow Him, we will have a perfect leading.
- It seems as if the lamps were cleaned and lit twice a day, at the time of the morning sacrifice (9 a.m.) and the evening sacrifice (3 p.m.).
- They gave light over against the Table of Shewbread and the Altar of Incense. In fact, as stated, this was the only light provided in the Holy Place.
- The *"tongs"* and the *"snuff dishes"* had to do with the cleaning of the wick, or replacing the wick, in order that the light might burn clean and bright.
- A talent of pure gold weighed about 120 pounds. At 16 ounces to the pound, we come up with 1,920 ounces. At $1,500 per ounce, we have a total of about $2,880,000, which would have been the present cost of gold, as it regards the Lampstand. This would not have included the craftsmanship that it took to make the sacred vessel.
- Moses was instructed to follow the pattern exactly, which means it was not to be deviated from in any capacity.

THE PATTERN

This tells us that the work of the Spirit in our hearts and lives must be carried out strictly on God's terms and His terms alone. The moment we begin to tamper with this which the Lord has done, in other words, to tamper with His plan, at that moment, we destroy the work of God in our lives. Regrettably, this is the great sin of the church.

His *"pattern"* is the Cross and our faith in that finished work. We must understand that the moment we attempt to put our own strength and ability into the mix, we have wrecked the victory that we could have. The Holy Spirit will not function in that capacity whatsoever. He demands that we exhibit faith exclusively in Christ and the Cross, which gives Him the ability to work within our lives, and which guarantees victory in every capacity. In this manner and this manner alone, we can have what we should have in the Lord as believers, which refers to victory over the world, the flesh, and the Devil (Rom. 6:3-14; 8:1-11; I Cor. 1:17-18, 21, 23; 2:2; Col. 2:10-15).

"There is a Fountain open for my cleansing,
"Where sin's atonement by my Lord was made;
"He was the Lamb who was led to the slaughter,
"His blood the fountain where my debt was paid."

"There is a Rock that stands by storms unshaken,
"Redemption's author the foundation laid;
"By faith my stand on His righteousness I've taken,
"He will not fail; I shall not be dismayed."

"There is a Book that points the path to glory,
"Eternal guidepost for the wayward soul;
"On its fair pages is told the wondrous story
"Of life in Christ the everlasting goal."

"There is a Hope, a wondrous consolation,
"In a benighted world a constant star;
"These eyes now dulled by the shadows that surround me,
"My Saviour shall behold in realms afar."

"There is a Home my Saviour is preparing,
"I may not need to cross death's sullen vale;
"Soon from earth's bondage His coming will release me,
"To live where joys eternal shall prevail."

10

The Ark of the Covenant

CHAPTER TEN

The Ark of the Covenant

"AND THEY SHALL make an ark of shittim wood: two cubits and a half shall be the length thereof, and a cubit and a half the breadth thereof, and a cubit and a half the height thereof" (Ex. 25:10).

The *"Ark of the Covenant"* occupies a leading place in the divine communications to Moses. Its position, too, in the Tabernacle was most marked. Shut in within the Veil in the Holiest of all, it formed the base of Jehovah's throne, so to speak. An ark, so far as the Word instructs us, is designed to preserve intact whatever is put therein. When, therefore, we read of the Ark of the Covenant, we are led to believe that it was designed by God to preserve His Covenant unbroken in the midst of an erring people.

But yet, as far as man was concerned, the Brazen Altar was the most important vessel given to Moses in the pattern. It alone, which represented Christ and His atoning work, could get man to the Holiest of Holies. In other words, the high priest dared not go into the Holy of Holies without first going to the Brazen Altar and offering up sacrifice in order to take the blood into the Ark of the Covenant containing the Mercy Seat.

THE DIMENSIONS

Counting 18 inches to the cubit, the Ark was about three feet and nine inches long, two feet and three inches wide, and two feet and three inches high.

The Ark was made at Sinai by Bezaleel, as we shall see, to the pattern given to Moses. It was used as a depository for the written Law (Deut. 31:9; Josh. 24:26) and played a significant part at the crossing of Jordan (Josh., Chpts. 3-4), the fall of Jericho (Josh., Chpt. 6), and the ceremony of remembering the covenant at Mount Ebal (Josh. 8:30).

From Gilgal, the Ark was moved to Bethel (Judg. 2:1; 20:27) but was taken to Shiloh in the time of the judges (I Sam. 1:3; 3:3), remaining there until captured by the Philistines on the battlefield at Ebenezer (I Sam., Chpt. 4). Because its presence caused seven months of plagues, the Philistines returned it to Kirjath-jearim, where it remained at least for 20 years, and possibly much longer (I Sam. 7:2).

DAVID

David installed the Ark in a tent at Jerusalem when he became king (II Sam., Chpt. 6) and would not remove it during Absalom's rebellion (II Sam. 15:24-29). It was placed in the Temple with great ceremony in the reign of Solomon (I Ki. 8:1) and remained in the Sanctuary up unto, and through, Josiah's reforms (II Chron. 35:3), when Jeremiah anticipated an age without its presence (Jer. 3:16).

It is believed by the Jews that immediately before the invasion by the Babylonians, Jeremiah took the Ark out of the Holy of Holies in the Temple and hid it in a cave. This was in 587 B.C. However, it has never been found from then until now. There was no Ark in the second Temple, and neither was there an Ark in the Temple built by Herod, in which Jesus ministered.

ISRAEL

Israel was chosen by God to be the leading nation in the world, in fact, the nation that would lead all other nations to righteousness, i.e., to God. Regrettably, Israel failed terribly, with the scepter of power being taken from her and given to the Gentiles. The first Gentile power was Babylon. That scepter of power now rests with the United States.

After the Rapture of the church, this power will pass to the Antichrist. Jesus said concerning the Jewish people: *"And they shall fall by the edge of the sword, and shall be led away captive into all nations (this took place in 70 A.D., and continued for many, many centuries): and Jerusalem shall be trodden down of the Gentiles (in a sense that continues to remain so, and will have its climax during the time of the Antichrist), until the times of the Gentiles be fulfilled"* (Lk. 21:24).

The *"times of the Gentiles"* will come to an end at the Second Coming of Christ, with Israel then accepting Him as Lord, Messiah, and Saviour. She will then be restored and once again given her place as the leader of nations (Ezek., Chpts. 40-48; Rev., Chpt. 19).

SHITTIM WOOD

As we said in one of the headings, this was referred to at times as indestructible wood. It was a type of wood that insects would not invade, and it would not rot. It came from the acacia tree.

It represented the perfect, pure, unsullied, physical body of our Lord Jesus Christ, which was perfected for sacrifice.

THE GOLD AND THE CROWN

"And you shall overlay it with pure gold, within and without shall you overlay it, and shall make upon it a crown of gold round about" (Ex. 25:11).

The core of the making of the Tabernacle is found in Chapters 25 through 30. This section, as we shall see, contains two parts.

THE GOLD AND THE CROWN

If it is to be noticed, the description begins with the Ark, which represents the throne of God. We see Christ descending from that throne, pictured in Chapters 25 through 27, to the Brazen Altar, that is, Calvary. This proclaims the gracious out coming of God to meet the sinner.

Williams said, *"Chapters 28 through 30 present man, in symbol, drawing near to God in the person of the Great High Priest. Thus the first half of this section of Exodus begins with the Ark, and moves outward to the Brazen Altar; the second, begins with the Brazen Altar and moves inward to the Ark."*

THE INCARNATION

The Ark was overlaid with pure gold, both within and without. This represented the fact that Christ was and is God. It covered the shittim wood, which represented His humanity. Thus, He was the God-Man, Jesus Christ.

This doesn't mean that He was half man and half God, for that is basely incorrect. He was fully God and fully man. As one Greek scholar said, *"When our Lord became man, He laid aside the expression of His deity, while never losing possession of His deity."* While He was fully man, at the same time, He was fully God!

The *"crown of gold round about the Ark,"* represented His status as king.

As we have stated and will continue to state, everything about the Tabernacle — its materials, its furniture, its vessels, everything within and everything without — symbolized the person, the atoning work, the ministries, the glories, and the perfections of Christ as Jehovah's perfect servant and as the Saviour and high priest of His people.

THE STAVES

"And you shall cast four rings of gold for it, and put them in the four corners thereof; and two rings shall be in the one side of it, and two rings in the other side of it.

"And you shall make staves of shittim wood, and overlay them with gold.

"And you shall put the staves into the rings by the sides of the Ark, that the Ark may be borne with them.

"The staves shall be in the rings of the Ark: they shall not be taken from it" (Ex. 25:12-15).

The four golden rings, two on each side, were placed there for staves to be inserted so the Ark could be transported when Israel moved. This spoke of her wilderness experience. This represented the fact that the Ark of the Covenant was to accompany the people in all their wanderings in the wilderness, which typified the world.

As well, it typified the fact that God desired to be with His people, despite the fact that they were an erring people.

However, the Ark was not always to be moved from place to place, hence, the staves would ultimately be drawn out, and we speak of the coming time when the Temple would be built.

The afflictions of David, as well as the wars of Israel, were to ultimately have an end. The prayer was yet to be breathed and answered, *"Arise, O Lord, into Your rest. You and the Ark of Your strength"* (Ps. 132:8).

DRAW OUT THE STAVES

This petition would have its partial accomplishment in the days of Solomon when the priests would bring the Ark of the

Covenant into the House of the Lord, place it under the giant Cherubim, and then would draw out the staves (I Ki. 8:6-8). However, this would be approximately 600 years in coming.

Solomon's Temple, incidentally, and the situation of Israel at that time foreshadowed the coming Kingdom Age when all will be at rest.

The fact that the *"staves"* were not to be taken from the Ark, at least at the time of its wanderings, suggests the fact that there be no need of touching even the rings, much less the Ark, when it was set down or taken up. The bearers were to take hold of the staves only, which were actually no part of the Ark. We can see from II Sam. 6:6-7 the danger of touching the Ark.

Thank God, that danger has been removed, symbolically speaking, by what Jesus did at the Cross, thereby, opening up the way that all may come, *"without money and without price"* (Isa. 55:1).

Since the Cross, we now enjoy the privilege of Christ dwelling within us by and through the power, agency, ministry, and person of the Holy Spirit. Still, this Tabernacle of the believer groans for redemption and the coming of the Lord, which will then place us literally with Christ, and will do so forever (Rom. 8:23).

THE TESTIMONY

"And you shall put into the Ark the Testimony which I shall give you" (Ex. 25:16).

This is undoubtedly the two tables of stone, written with the finger of God, and forming His testimony against sin (Deut. 31:26-27).

This seems to have been the main purpose of the Ark, the containing of the Testimony. Of course, it pictures Christ fully and totally keeping the Law in every respect and, in fact, He was the only One who was able to accomplish this great task. However, it must always be remembered that He did all of this as our representative man, i.e., *"the Second Man"* (I Cor. 15:47). Simple faith in what He did for us at the Cross gives us His perfection, i.e., *"perfect law-keeping,"* thereby, making us, in the eyes of God, and all because of Christ, perfect lawkeepers. The believer must ever understand that all of this represented Christ in what He would do in His redemptive work, in actuality, what He would do for us. Let us never forget that everything He did was all done, in its entirety, for sinners, i.e., *for us.* So, doesn't it make sense, especially considering the great price that He paid, that we should have all that He has done for us? To be sure, we can have it all, but only in one way.

FAITH

All of these wonderful things which He has done for us can be obtained in only one way, and that is by faith (Eph. 2:8-9; Heb. 11:5-6). However, when we use the word *"faith,"* always and without exception, we are referring to faith in Christ and what He did for us at the Cross. As we repeatedly state, if we separate Christ from His Cross, where the great price was paid, the faith we then exhibit, God cannot honor. The faith He honors, and the only faith He honors, is found in the words of Paul, *"We preach Christ crucified"* (I Cor. 1:23). If we attempt to separate Christ from the Cross, which means to abandon the Cross, or even to minimize it in any way, we then do violence to the Word of God, which finds us then worshipping and serving *"another Jesus"* (II Cor. 11:4).

ANOTHER JESUS?

What in the world did Paul mean by statements such as *"another Jesus," "another spirit,"* and *"another gospel"*? As stated, we find this in II Cor. 11:4.

He was speaking of preaching Jesus without emphasizing the Cross (I Cor. 1:17-18, 21, 23; 2:2). Regrettably, that's the sin of the modern church. It lauds Jesus, but it's Jesus without the Cross.

Let all and sundry know and understand that if we preach *"Jesus Christ and Him crucified,"* we will, at the same time, have Jesus as the healer, Jesus as the provider, Jesus as the baptizer with the Holy Spirit, etc. It is the Cross of Christ that makes all of this possible, but if we preach Jesus without the Cross, we will not only lose salvation, but we will lose all the other as well!

If *"Jesus and Him crucified"* is properly preached, not only will people be saved, but healing will occur, financial provision will be made, believers will be baptized with the Holy Spirit with the evidence of speaking with other tongues, and we will have peace and grace, as well as the fruit and gifts of the Spirit. However, take a look at the modern church!

Christ and the Cross are not being preached, and, as well, people aren't being saved, people aren't being healed, people aren't being delivered, and the *"fruit"* and the *"gifts"* are but a distant memory — all because the Cross is being denied or ignored.

Oh, yes, all types of miracles are being claimed, etc., but if close inspection is made, we find that most of the claims are empty and hollow!

"From Calvary a cry was heard,
"A bitter and heart-rending cry;
"My Saviour! Every mournful word
"Bespeaks Your soul's deep agony."

"A horror of great darkness fell
"On You, You spotless, Holy One!
"And all the swarming hosts of hell,
"Conspired to tempt God's only Son."

"The scourge, the thorns, the deep disgrace,
"These You could bear, not once repine;
"But when Jehovah vailed His face,
"Unutterable pangs were Thine."

"Let the dumb world its silence break;
"Let pealing anthems rend the sky;
"Awake my sluggish soul, awake!
"He died, that we might never die."

"Lord! On Your cross I fix my eye;
"If e're I lose its strong control,
"Oh let that dying, piercing cry,
"Melt and reclaim my wandering soul."

11
The Mercy Seat

CHAPTER ELEVEN

The Mercy Seat

"AND YOU SHALL make a Mercy Seat of pure gold, two cubits and a half shall be the length thereof, and a cubit and a half the breadth thereof" (Ex. 25:17).

The Mercy Seat formed the covering for the Ark of the Covenant. On it was sprinkled the atoning blood, which the high priest did once a year, on the Great Day of Atonement. It was of this blood-sprinkled Mercy Seat that God spoke when He said, *"There will I meet with you."* Here in type was the only meeting place between God and the sinner. Here, righteousness and peace kissed each other. God demands, and the sinner needs, a spotless righteousness. This is found only in the Cross of Christ. At this blood-sprinkled Mercy Seat, God is perfectly glorified, and the believer eternally saved.

The dimensions of the Mercy Seat were the same as the Ark regarding length and width. It is believed to have been about one inch thick or possibly more. It was made out of pure gold, typifying that mercy and grace are all of God and none of man.

Gold is very heavy, and it is believed that such a slab would be about 75 pounds. If that were, in fact, the case, the Mercy Seat made of pure gold would have been worth nearly $1.8 million in 2014 money.

The Mercy Seat differed from the Ark, as is obvious, in that no wood entered into its composition. There was only one other piece of furniture in the Tabernacle made solely of gold, namely the Lampstand, which was smaller in size and weight; therefore, this part of the Mercy Seat, according to its intrinsic worth, was the most valuable of all the holy vessels. This speaks to us of the preciousness in the sight of God of that which the Mercy Seat foreshadowed.

PROPITIATION

The Mercy Seat derived its name from the blood of propitiation, which was sprinkled on it.

The word *"propitiation"* means *"that which atones,"* in this case, the blood.

"Atone" or *"atonement"* means *"to supply satisfaction, to expatiate, to make amends, to reconcile, to pay the price."*

Paul explained this in New Testament terms by saying: **"Even the righteousness of God** (*the Law of God*) **which is by faith of Jesus Christ** (*the perfect righteousness of God gained by anyone who expresses faith in Christ*) **unto all and upon all of them who believe** (*excluding none*)**: for there is no difference:**

"For all have sinned, and come short of the glory of God (*meaning that none can have this righteousness without faith in Christ*)**:**

"**Being justified freely by His grace through the redemption that is in Christ Jesus** (*having faith in Christ and what He did for us at the Cross*):

"**Whom God has set forth to be a propitiation** (*atonement*) **through faith in His blood** (*we can only have this righteousness by exhibiting faith in Christ and what He did for us at the Cross*), **to declare His righteousness** (*the perfect righteousness of Christ*) **for the remission of sins that are past** (*past, present, and future*) **through the forbearance of God** (*leniency*);

"**To declare, I say, at this time His righteousness: that He might be just** (*demanding justice, which was rendered by Christ*), **and the justifier of him who believes in Jesus**" (*which God can do, because His holiness and righteousness have been satisfied in Christ*) (**Rom. 3:22-26**).

THE PRICE IS PAID

In this statement, the Holy Spirit through Paul bears testimony to the fact that God's blessed Son is the One by whom the Father was propitiated, the One by whom His holy wrath against the sins of His people was pacified, the One by whom the righteous demands of His law were satisfied, and the One by whom every attribute of deity was glorified.

The *"type"* of Christ as *"the propitiation* (satisfaction) *for our sins"* is the bleeding victim on the Altar; the *"type"* of Christ as God's resting place or propitiatory (God's demands are satisfied) is the Mercy Seat within the Veil. Christ has become God's rest in whom He can now meet poor sinners in all the fullness of His grace because of the propitiation made by Him on the Cross.

In effect, Christ is the *"Mercy Seat,"* but He is so by virtue of the propitiation (satisfaction) which He offered to God.

To make it easier to understand, Jesus Christ died on the Cross, thereby, paying the price for all sin, past, present, and future, at least for all who will believe (Jn. 3:16). Thus, He satisfied the demands of a thrice-holy God, who had demanded satisfaction, and who received satisfaction in what Christ did at the Cross.

Consequently, for all who place their faith and trust in Christ and what He did at the Cross, thereby, believing that His precious shed blood at the Cross atoned for all sin, deliverance from all sin will be granted, and eternal life will be given (Jn. 3:16; Gal. 1:4).

While the Bible does not teach sinless perfection, it most definitely does teach that sin (the sin nature) is not to have dominion over us (Rom. 6:14).

Thank God, it is a *mercy seat* and not a *judgment seat!*

THE IMPORTANCE OF THE MERCY SEAT

In our understanding of salvation, and especially our understanding of Christ, we must realize that it is impossible to overestimate the importance of God's satisfaction in Christ. In other words, the price that Christ paid, the work that He accomplished, and the great Plan of Redemption, even planned before the foundation of the world, have all been completely brought about in totality due to what Christ did at the Cross. The blood was applied to the Mercy Seat, typifying the blood that would be shed by Christ, which would appease the wrath of God against sin and forever portray the debt as having been paid. In other words, all the sinner has to do in order to be saved is to simply place his faith and trust exclusively in Christ and what Christ did for him at the Cross, and salvation will be instant (Jn. 3:16; Eph. 2:8-9; Rev. 22:17).

This means that the believing sinner must understand that his good works merit him nothing! His religiosity merits him nothing! In fact, there is nothing that God will accept other than our faith in Christ and His atoning work.

As it regards our sanctification, and I speak of the believer's growth in Christ, the Mercy Seat also is linked closely to the Altar of Incense. Perhaps it would be better to say that the Altar of Incense, which we have studied, is linked very closely to the Mercy Seat.

THE DIMENSIONS OF THE MERCY SEAT

The Mercy Seat fit exactly on the top of the Ark of the Covenant. It was not smaller, and it was not wider. If it is to be noticed, the Mercy Seat was too cubits and one-half long, exactly as the Ark of the Covenant. As well, it was one cubit and one-half in width, exactly as the Ark.

There was a reason for this, as should be obvious. Some attempt to make the Mercy Seat wider than the Ark, but this is a vain delusion. What do we mean by that?

In other words, they are claiming things other than the blood of Christ, but let all and sundry understand that no grace can be shown to any sinner apart from the redemptive blood of the Lord Jesus. Saving mercy is extended to none except those who accept Christ, who alone met the demands of divine justice.

Let it be understood that Christ died not only to make possible the salvation of the whole human race, even though most will not accept, but also to make certain the salvation of those who come to Him. The Scripture says: *"All who the Father gives Me, shall come to Me* (shall come by Me, for that's the only way anyone can come)*: and him who comes to Me, I will in no wise cast out"* (Jn. 6:37).

There are some who claim, perhaps many, that the love of God will save them, despite the fact that they have rejected Christ. Such hope can only be classified as a fool's hope. There is no salvation outside of Christ, as there can be no salvation outside of Christ.

THE LAW

The primary reason that Christ came to this world was that the Law of God, which was God's standard of righteousness, and which standard He must uphold, might be met in totality and kept faithfully, which it was by Christ. As well, He not only kept the Law perfectly, but He also satisfied the demands of the broken Law. This included every human being who had ever lived, and who would live in the future. He did so by the sacrificial offering of Himself on the Cross of Calvary, which paid it all.

That is the connection by the Mercy Seat with the Ark of the Covenant. In that Ark was kept the two stones which contained the Ten Commandments, which, incidentally, had been repeatedly broken by man. So, the Mercy Seat, fitting exactly the Ark of the Covenant, and especially the blood applied to the Mercy Seat, stated unequivocally that the Law had been satisfied. When God would look at the Mercy Seat, instead of seeing the broken Law, He would see the blood, hence, Him saying, as it regards the Children of Israel being

delivered from Egyptian bondage, *"When I see the blood, I will pass over you"* (Ex. 12:13). This was the criterion even before the Law or instructions regarding the Tabernacle were given, even beginning with the first family (Gen., Chpt. 4). It hasn't changed from then until now. The Mercy Seat with the applied blood, the blood of Christ, still says to all of mankind, *"When I see the blood, I will pass over you."* This means that the judgment of God will pass you by because you are safely protected by the blood of the Lamb.

CHERUBIM

"And you shall make two Cherubim of gold, of beaten work shall you make them, in the two ends of the Mercy Seat.

"And make one Cherub on the one end, and the other Cherub on the other end: even of the Mercy Seat shall you make the Cherubim on the two ends thereof.

"And the Cherubim shall stretch forth their wings on high, covering the Mercy Seat with their wings, and their faces shall look one to another; toward the Mercy Seat shall the faces of the Cherubim be" (Ex. 25:18-20).

The phrase, *"Of beaten work shall you make them,"* records the fact that these strange creatures, made of gold, were not attached to the ends of the Mercy Seat but were actually a part of the Mercy Seat. In other words, the Mercy Seat and the two Cherubs were all one piece of gold, and it was not merely gold plating, but rather pure gold. So, regarding the gold and the craftsmanship, if one would attempt to estimate the cost presently, this one item could easily have cost some $4 million or more! However, it's hardly worthwhile to mention money in connection with this.

The two Cherubs looked down on the Mercy Seat, in effect, on the Law which had been grossly broken by man. Of course, as stated, when the blood was applied by the high priest once a year, then the blood would be seen instead of the broken Law, which was the idea!

WHAT DID THESE CHERUBS LOOK LIKE?

Cherubim are mentioned for the first time in Scripture in Genesis 3:24. They are seen there as guarding the way to the Tree of Life, and doing so with a *"flaming sword."* This seems to suggest that they have to do with God's judicial authority.

In Revelation 4:6-8, we find them related to the throne of God; and quite possibly, they might be the highest among the angelic order, or at least in the capacity in which they function.

While the ones described by John in the book of Revelation are not referred to as *"Cherubim,"* but rather as *"Living Creatures,"* it is almost certain that Cherubim are meant. And yet, in Isaiah, Chapter 6, we have angelic beings referred to as *"Seraphim,"* which are very similar to the description given to those in John's vision. Both say, *"Holy, Holy, Holy"*

(Isa. 6:2-3; Rev. 4:8). It seems that each has six wings, and they both are at the throne of God.

A DIFFERENT FACE

In John's vision, these Living Creatures each had a different face: that of a man, a flying eagle, a lion, and a calf. Isaiah doesn't say what the face of the Seraphim looks like. We do know that these strange creatures do not add to the holiness of God, but that they rather proclaim His holiness. By crying *"Holy, Holy, Holy,"* they proclaim the fact that the Creator is a thrice-Holy God. This is the reason that sinful man cannot approach Him, except in one capacity, and that is by and through Christ, especially His shed blood.

THE CHERUBIM

Oh dear reader, do you not sense the presence of God even as we attempt to lift up Christ and the great price that He paid? Do you not realize how sinful and wicked it is to deny His Cross, to ignore His Cross, or even to minimize the significance of His Cross? Even if we pay lip service to the Cross but register unbelief by our actions, that can be construed as none other than hypocrisy. What do I mean by that?

MAN'S SUBSTITUTE FOR THE CROSS

Back in the late 1800s, Sigmund Freud, a man who didn't know God, and, in fact, who was bound by vices of immorality, instituted what is referred to now as humanistic psychology. It is the attempt of the world, nurtured and fostered by the Evil One himself, to meet the needs of man in a way other than by Christ and what Christ did at the Cross. Actually, one might refer to humanistic psychology as the religion of humanism.

Regrettably, about 30 or 40 years after Freud made his debut, during which time this philosophy girdled the globe, many in the church, who had strayed and drifted from the biblical way, began to embrace this evil, and evil it is!

By the 1940s, most in the denominational world had embraced this means and method almost completely. By the 1950s, sadly and regrettably, the Pentecostal denominations, which were already beginning to lose their way, began to accept this vain philosophy a nibble at a time.

At the present time, the acceptance of humanistic psychology is almost total as it regards the church, irrespective of its stripe. For instance, the Assemblies of God advocate that if a person has a problem, he should seek out a good 12-step program, which, of course, as all know, at least who know anything at all about psychology, is the method of claimed help. As well, the Church of God (Cleveland, Tennessee), the second largest Pentecostal denomination, has embraced this system in totality. Actually, in attempting to attain to higher education, almost all Church of God preachers major in psychology.

THE OPPOSITE OF THE WAY OF THE CROSS

If anyone knows anything at all about psychology, he knows that this humanistic way is the total opposite of the way of the Cross. Despite the fact that the practitioners of this shamanism, and a shamanism it is, try to meld the two, the two ways are poles apart. Either Jesus addressed at the Cross every problem that grips humanity, or else He didn't. I happen to believe that He did because the Bible says He did (Col. 2:10-15), and I know from personal experience that He did.

Humanistic psychology has never set one single captive free. Every single soul in this world, who has ever been set free from the bondages of sin in any capacity, has been set free by Christ and what Christ has done for us at the Cross. To be sure, Christ needs no help! As we have stated, the Mercy Seat fits exactly the top of the Ark of the Covenant. It is not too little or too big.

THE CATHOLIC CHURCH

All are aware of the problem that plagues the Catholic Church as it regards the molestation of little boys by Catholic priests. Actually, the priesthood of the Catholic Church is a haven for homosexuals. The homosexual by satanic nature is a predator. To be sure, young boys are the victims highest on their list. Regrettably, once molested, many of these young boys turn out to be homosexuals themselves.

I said all of that to say this: the Catholic Church has long since majored in humanistic psychology; in fact, not knowing the Lord at all, humanistic psychology is their mainstay. Consequently, they have some of the best psychologists in the world.

If psychology is the answer, then why isn't it helping these Catholic priests, many of them who have gone through every type of psychological therapy available?

It hasn't helped them simply because there is no help from that source. So, what am I saying in all of this?

HAVE CEASED TO BE OF ANY USE TO GOD

I'm saying that the Pentecostal denominations, in America and Canada, who once knew the power of the Holy Spirit, have now, for all practical purposes, abandoned the Cross of Christ. While they may continue to pay lip service to the Cross, their actions speak louder than their words.

To be sure, the statements I've just made are at least one of the reasons that these denominations strongly detest Jimmy Swaggart. I regret that! However, as much as I regret that, I will not cease to tell the truth. My ministry is not for sale, and, in fact, it has never been for sale. Pure and simple, these particular denominations, for all practical purposes, have ceased to be of any use to God whatsoever. While there is an exception here and there among their preachers and churches, as a whole, what I'm saying is true. The reason can be boiled down to the fact that they have abandoned the Cross of Christ. Until they come back to the Cross, their spiritual deterioration will only tend to accelerate. Those Cherubs are still looking down upon the Mercy Seat, and they are still saying, *"Holy, Holy, Holy."* The only way that mankind can escape the *"flaming sword"* is by full and total acceptance of the blood that was placed on the Mercy Seat. It is still, *"When I see the blood, I will pass over you."* That has not changed, and that will never change!

As for me and my house, we will stick with what that great Apostle Simon Peter said nearly 2,000 years ago: *"Grace and peace be multiplied unto you through the knowledge of God, and of Jesus our Lord,*

"According as His divine power has given unto us all things that pertain unto life and godliness, through the knowledge of Him who has called us to glory and virtue:

"Whereby are given unto us exceeding great and precious promises: that by these you might be partakers of the divine nature, having escaped the corruption that is in the world through lust" (II Pet. 1:2-4).

COMMUNICATION

"And you shall put the Mercy Seat above upon the Ark; and in the Ark you shall put the Testimony that I shall give you.

"And there will I meet with you, and I will commune with you from above the Mercy Seat, from between the two Cherubim which are upon the Ark of the Testimony, of all things which I will give you in commandment unto the Children of Israel" (Ex. 25:21-22).

Thank God, the Mercy Seat is above the Ark of the Covenant, which contains the Law with the demands that it be kept by me and every other human being, but which we are woefully inadequate to comply. I don't care how great you may think your faith might be, and I don't care how many gifts of the Spirit may function through you; if your faith is not properly placed in the Cross, you simply cannot live an overcoming, victorious Christian life, irrespective as to whom you might be. The Cross is typified by the blood on the Mercy Seat, the blood shed by Christ on Calvary.

Point out to me the preacher over television whom the church thinks is mightily used of God, and if that brother or sister doesn't understand the manner in which the Holy Spirit works, he or she is living a life of spiritual failure. This is true irrespective of the fact that he or she may be drawing gigantic crowds and claiming all types of miracles. When we say that a person doesn't understand the manner in which the Holy Spirit works, we are referring to the believer anchoring his faith in the finished work of Christ, which gives the Holy Spirit latitude to work. It cannot be otherwise! God has only one remedy for sin — not 10, not five, not two — just one, and that is the Cross of Christ.

THE CROSS

If you, the reader, are wearied by my constant repetition regarding the Cross, approaching this subject in every way that I can, then this proves that you do not properly understand the Cross as you should. I would advise you to earnestly seek the Lord that He might reveal to you this foundational truth. If you will be honest and earnest before Him, I will assure you that this is a prayer He will answer.

The latter portion of Verse 21, about putting the Testimony (Ten Commandments) into the Ark, is virtually the same as Verse 16, with the repetition intended by the Holy Spirit.

Anytime there is a repetition of this nature, and the Bible occasionally registers such, it is always done for purpose and reason. The Holy Spirit is endeavoring to draw our attention to something that is very important. So, what is important about this particular statement?

The Lord is telling us here that the Ten Commandments, referred to as the *"Testimony,"* is the moral Law of God. It is God's standard of righteousness, that which He demands that man keep, and must do so without breaking it even one time.

Some have claimed in these last few years that God has set the standard too high. No, the standard is not too high. The problem is, man's moral strength is too low. Lowering the standard will not help; in fact, it will only exacerbate the matter. A thrice-holy God, symbolized by the Cherubim, cannot accept less than total and complete perfection. When we say perfection, we're not speaking of perfection for a short period of time, but perfection constantly.

Sadly, this shoots man down before he even begins, for the simple reason that man is conceived in sin and born in sin. We're speaking of original sin, which is the state of the human race because of Adam's fall. Paul explained to us how this happened.

THE APOSTLE PAUL

He said: *"For since by man* (Adam) *came death* (the Fall) *by man* (Christ Jesus) *came also the resurrection of the dead.*

"For as in Adam all die (died spiritually and physically) *even so in Christ shall all be made alive"* (I Cor. 15:21-22).

So, due to the Fall, man in his weakened moral condition simply cannot attain to the level which God demands, and demand it He does. However, there is a way out of this dilemma, portrayed to us by the Mercy Seat.

God would become man, the Man Christ Jesus, and as our substitute, would do for man what man could not do for himself. He would be born under the Law (Gal. 4:4), but without original sin, because He wasn't conceived by man and was born of the Virgin Mary.

He kept the Law perfectly in every respect, all on our behalf as our substitute. However, not only did He do that, He, as well, suffered the curse and penalty of the broken Law, which condemned every human being, thereby, redeeming us from that curse, *"being made a curse for us"* (Gal. 3:13).

So, the Holy Spirit telling Moses that the Testimony must be placed in the Ark is, in fact, telling us that these Commandments are the moral Laws of God and must be kept and, in fact, were kept by Christ Jesus, and Christ Jesus alone!

COMMUNION

Verse 22 tells us:

- It is only above the bloodstained Mercy Seat that God will meet with sinful human beings because that's the only place that He can meet with sinful human beings and not malign His righteousness and holiness. Now, let the reader understand that.

When John, in his great vision given in Revelation, Chapters 4 and 5, saw the throne of God, the Scripture says, *"And I beheld, and, lo, in the midst of the throne and of the four living creatures, and in the midst of the elders, stood a*

Lamb as it had been slain, having seven horns, and seven eyes, which are the seven Spirits of God sent forth into all the earth" (Rev. 5:6).

The elders whom John saw, which represent all the redeemed of the earth, are able to stand at the throne of God all because of the *"slain Lamb."*

The Cross is the meeting place between God and man. It is the point where grace and righteousness meet and perfectly harmonize. Nothing but perfect righteousness could suit God, and nothing but perfect grace could suit the sinner. However, where could these attributes meet in one point? Only at the Cross. There it is that *"Mercy and truth are met together; righteousness and peace have kissed each other"* (Ps. 85:10).

A TESTIMONY

Concerning this, C.H. Mackintosh said: *"Thus it is that the soul of the believing sinner finds peace. He sees that God's righteousness and His justification rest upon precisely the same basis, namely Christ's accomplished work. When man, under the powerful action of the truth of God, takes his place as a sinner, God can, in the exercise of grace, take His place as a Savior, and then every question is settled, for the Cross having answered all the claims of divine justice, mercy's copious streams can flow unhindered. When a righteous God and a ruined sinner meet on a blood-sprinkled platform, all is settled forever — settled in such a way as perfectly glorifies God, and eternally saves the sinner."*

He then said, *"When man is so thoroughly brought down to the lowest point of his own moral condition before God, as to be willing to take the place which God's truth assigns him, he then learns that God has revealed Himself as the Righteous Justifier of such an one."*

THE FINISHED WORK OF CHRIST

- It is through the finished work of Christ on the Cross, typified by the Mercy Seat, that not only will the Lord meet with fallen man, but it is, as well, where He will fellowship with man, and there alone. In fact, the Cross (Mercy Seat) is the only place where God will meet with fallen man.

This tells us that if a man attempts to come to God any way other than the bloodstained Cross, he will be frozen out. In fact, the Holy Spirit forever stands guard to keep out those who would attempt to reach God in any manner other than the Cross.

Listen to what Paul said: *"But now in Christ Jesus you who sometimes were far off are made nigh by the blood of Christ ... For through Him we both* (Jews and Gentiles) *have access by one Spirit* (the Holy Spirit) *unto the Father"* (Eph. 2:13, 18).

This tells us that access to the throne of God, to the grace of God, and, in fact, to all that God is, is gained only by one way, and that is by the Cross of Christ and our faith in that finished work. The Holy Spirit guarantees access for all who come by that route but, at the same time, guarantees that the door will be closed to all who attempt to come another way. When Jesus said, *"I am the door,"* He was speaking of a blood-splattered door, typified by the houses in Egypt where the blood was applied (Jn. 10:9; Ex. 12:13).

All of this typifies the throne of God and the way — the only way that man can approach Him — which is by and through the Cross of Christ. That's the reason I'm so insistent upon the Cross! That's the reason I approach this subject from every angle that the Lord gives me! That's the reason I address it in every fashion that I know how, even to the place of being overly repetitive. I do so because man can meet God in no other manner than by the Cross.

The two Cherubim speak of the holiness of God, and the Testimony, as we have stated, speaks of the standard of God, which is the Ten Commandments.

THE TESTIMONY

Because of man's inability to keep the Commandments, Paul said, and rightly so, that these things were against us. This means that man broke the Ten Commandments, which means that he didn't obey God and incurred upon himself a terrible penalty.

Paul said, *"Blotting out the handwriting of ordinances that was against us, which was contrary to us, and took it out of the way, nailing it to His Cross"* (Col. 2:14).

Jesus satisfied the curse and the penalty of the broken Law, which was death, and did so by the giving of Himself in sacrifice (Gal. 1:4).

To be sure, He alone could pay this price because He alone was perfect, consequently, the only sacrifice that God would accept.

Under the old Jewish Law, which we are now studying, the man bringing the animal for sacrifice was accepted by God on the basis of the sacrifice being accepted. In other words, if the sacrifice was approved, then the one offering the sacrifice was approved. It is no different now.

Our faith in Christ and what Christ has done for us at the Cross guarantees our acceptance simply because God has accepted Christ. Unfortunately, we get it backward many times, thinking that something we do makes us accepted. It doesn't! We are accepted only on the basis of our faith in Christ and what He did for us at the Cross because Christ has been accepted by God (Eph. 2:13-18).

> *"Oh, now I see the crimson wave*
> *"The fountain deep and wide;*
> *"Jesus my Lord, mighty to save,*
> *"Points to His wounded side."*

> *"I see the new creation rise,*
> *"I hear the speaking blood;*
> *"It speaks! Polluted nature dies*
> *"Sinks 'neath the crimson flood."*

> *"I rise to walk in heaven's own light,*
> *"Above the world and sin;*
> *"With hearts made pure and garments white,*
> *"And Christ enthroned within."*

> *"Amazing grace! 'Tis heaven below,*
> *"To feel the blood applied;*
> *"And Jesus, only Jesus know,*
> *"My Jesus crucified."*

12

The Gate and The Court

CHAPTER TWELVE

The Gate and The Court

"AND YOU SHALL make the Court of the Tabernacle: for the south side southward there shall be hangings for the Court of fine twined linen of an hundred cubits long for one side" (Ex. 27:9).

The Tabernacle stood in the Court. The Court consisted of a fence, which was 150 feet long and 75 feet wide, measuring 18 inches to the cubit. The height of the fence was seven and one-half feet (Ex. 27:18).

The fence was made of *"fine twined linen,"* which meant that it was snow white and typified, as previously stated, the perfect righteousness and life of our Lord and Saviour, Jesus Christ.

In effect, the Tabernacle was situated in the very midst of the encampment of Israel, at least where the terrain allowed such.

Immediately around the Court of the Tabernacle were the tents of the Levites. Beyond, but encircling them, were grouped the Twelve Tribes, three on either side, thus forming a square of vast extent.

The Tabernacle, therefore, formed the center of Israel's camp.

The Court foreshadowed Christ on earth tabernacling among men and accessible to all who sought Him, but His glory was beheld only by those who drew near in faith (Jn. 1:14).

As everything centered around the Tabernacle, everything must center around Christ, of which the Tabernacle is a type.

But yet, the smallness of the Court stands in contrast to the vastness of the camp, which numbered upwards of 3 million people. This contains more than a hint of the fewness of those, from among the crowds of professing Christians, who really enter into God's presence! God's *"flock"* is only a *"little one"* (Lk. 12:32); only the *"few"* are in the *"narrow way"* (Mat. 7:14). And yet, the clarion call still is *"whosoever will!"* (Rev. 22:17).

THE PLACEMENT OF THE TRIBES

All the tribes surrounding the Tabernacle were placed in order, in effect, that the Tabernacle was in the center of the gathering of Israel.

On the east were probably the three tribes of Manasseh, Benjamin, and Dan.

On the north were probably the tribes of Reuben, Judah, and Levi.

On the south were the three tribes of Simeon, Issachar, and Zebulun.

On the west were the three tribes of Gad, Asher, and Naphtali.

When the camp of Israel moved while in the wilderness, the tribe of Judah would always go first (Num. 10:14).

Actually, Judah means *"praise."* This means that Israel was led by praises to the Lord.

THE PILLARS

"And the twenty pillars thereof and their twenty sockets shall be of copper; the hooks of the pillars and their fillets shall be of silver.

"And likewise for the north side in length there shall be hangings of an hundred cubits long, and his twenty pillars and their twenty sockets of copper; the hooks of the pillars and their fillets of silver.

"And for the breadth of the Court on the west side shall be hangings of fifty cubits: their pillars ten, and their sockets ten.

"And the breadth of the Court on the east side eastward shall be fifty cubits.

"The hangings of one side of the gate shall be fifteen cubits: their pillars three, and their sockets three.

"And on the other side shall be hangings fifteen cubits: their pillars three, and their sockets three" (Ex. 27:10-15).

THE PILLARS

There were 60 pillars placed at intervals of five cubits all around the Court. This, as well, and I speak of one being placed every five cubits, speaks of the grace of God. Considering the number of pillars, it speaks of unlimited grace.

The grace of God is simply the goodness of God extended to undeserving man. That is about the simplest explanation, I think, which can be given.

God has always dealt with man by grace because that's the only way He can deal with man; however, the Cross made it possible for grace to be extended to undeserving man in a much more abundant manner. It's not that God now has more grace than He once had, for that's incorrect. The Cross has made it possible for God to dispense grace in a more abundant way.

So, the 60 pillars situated five cubits apart from each other signify not only that God dealt with man through the medium of grace but, as well, that abundant grace was coming, of which all of this was a type.

THE MATERIALS OF WHICH
THE PILLARS WERE MADE

It would seem from Verse 10 that the pillars were made of copper; however, in the original Hebrew in which this was written, there is indication that the modifying phrase *"of copper"* refers only to the sockets and not to the pillars.

Even though the Scripture doesn't say, more than likely, the pillars were made of shittim wood. The other pillars — and I speak of those used for the Door and for the support of the Veil — were all of wood; therefore, in the absence of any word to the contrary, we naturally conclude that these also were made of the same material.

If, in fact, the pillars were made of indestructible wood, that would have fit perfectly with the fine twined linen, signifying the righteousness of Christ, as it regards His humanity.

THE GATE OF THE COURT

"And for the Gate of the Court shall be an hanging of twenty cubits, of blue, and purple, and scarlet, and fine twined linen, wrought with needlework: and their pillars shall be four, and their sockets four" (Ex. 27:16).

The *"Gate"* to the outer Court was very similar to the Gate which opened into the Tabernacle and the Veil which hid the Holy of Holies. Each of them served as a door, hiding the interior from one approaching from the outside.

THE GATE OF THE COURT

All were made of the same materials, and the colors are mentioned in the same order.

The Gate that led into the Court was 30 feet wide. The total width of the enclosure on the east as well as the west was 75 feet. So, the Gate in front took up nearly half of the space.

Its colors of blue, purple, scarlet, and the fine twined linen portrayed Christ in every capacity. He alone is *"the Door!"*

So, the Israelite who came to the Brazen Altar with his offering had to pass through this Gate of the Court; the priest who placed incense on the Golden Altar had to enter by the Door of the Tabernacle; and the high priest who entered the Holy of Holies on the Day of Atonement had to do so through the Veil, thus realizing the thrice-repeated proof of the only way of access to God.

THE GATE MUST BE ENTERED

However, a gate or a door must be understood in the following fashion: it's not enough to have access to the Gate or Door; it's not even enough to recognize that it is the Gate or Door. The Gate or Door must be entered before one can reap the benefits therein. There are very specific demands that it be entered, or else, it is of no value.

As well, when the Israelite came through the Gate, the first thing he would see would be the Brazen Altar. In effect, the presence of the Altar stated that sinful man could go no further. The only way he could come at all was to offer up sacrifice on the Altar, which would typify the One who was to come and would give His life for lost humanity.

THE COURT AND THE HOLY PLACE

"All the pillars roundabout the Court shall be filleted with silver; their hooks shall be of silver, and their sockets of copper.

"The length of the Court shall be an hundred cubits, and the breadth fifty cubits everywhere, and the height five cubits of fine twined linen, and their sockets of copper.

"All the vessels of the Tabernacle, and all the service thereof, and all the pins thereof, and all the pins of the Court shall be of copper.

"And you shall command the Children of Israel, that they bring you pure oil olive beaten for the light to cause the lamp to burn always.

"In the Tabernacle of the congregation without the Veil, which is before the Testimony, Aaron and his sons shall order it from evening to morning before the Lord: it shall be a statute forever unto their generations on the behalf of the Children of Israel" (Ex. 27:17-21).

The Court was as far as the Israelite, other than the priests, could come, at least as it regarded the Tabernacle, and then only so far as the Brazen Altar. However, everything about the outer Court, as well as the Tabernacle, spoke of Christ in either His atoning, mediatorial or intercessory work, even down to the small pins, which were of copper. As always, this spoke of the judgment that He would undergo on our behalf.

"The Church's one foundation
"Is Jesus Christ her Lord;
"She is His new creation
"By water and the Word:
"From Heaven He came and sought her
"To be His holy bride;
"With His own blood He bought her,
"And for her life He died."

"Elect from every nation,
"Yet one o'er all the earth,
"Her charter of salvation,
"One Lord, one faith, one birth,
"One holy name she blesses,
"Partakes one holy food,
"And to one hope she presses,
"With every grace endued."

"Though with a scornful wonder,
"Men see her sore opprest,
"By schisms rent asunder,
"By heresies distrest,
"Yet saints their watch are keeping,
"Their cry goes up, 'How long?'
"And soon the night of weeping
"Shall be the morn of song."

"Mid toil, and tribulation,
"And tumult of her war,
"She waits the consummation
"Of peace forevermore;
"Till with the vision glorious
"Her longing eyes are blest,
"And the great Church victorious
"Shall be the Church at rest."

"Yet she on earth has union
"With God the Three in One,
"And mystic sweet communion
"With those whose rest is won:
"Oh happy ones and holy!
"Lord, give us grace that we,
"Like them the meek and lowly,
"On high may dwell with Thee."

13

The Priestly Garments

CHAPTER THIRTEEN

The Priestly Garments

AS WE MAKE a short study of the garments of the priests, we must understand that these are the only garments in history that were designed by the Holy Spirit, with the exception of the garments of skins which were provided for Adam and Eve immediately after the Fall (Gen. 3:21).

All the designs concerning the priestly garments were given to Moses by the Lord, and he was to adhere strictly to the design simply because every bit of it pictured Christ in some manner.

THE EPHOD

"And of the blue, and purple, and scarlet, they made cloths of service, to do service in the Holy Place, and made the holy garments for Aaron; as the Lord commanded Moses.

"And he made the ephod of gold, blue, and purple, and scarlet, and fine twined linen" (Ex. 39:1-2).

The *"Holy Place,"* the first room of the Tabernacle, presents the major service area of the priests. In this place was the Table of Shewbread, the Lampstand, and the Altar of Incense. As one came into the Holy Place, the Table sat on the right, the Lampstand on the left, and the Altar immediately in front of the Veil, which hid the Holy of Holies.

In fact, if one had stood outside of the Tabernacle immediately in front of the Brazen Altar, and the Tabernacle structure had been taken down, leaving the sacred vessels, they would have formed a perfect Cross. The Lampstand and the Table would have formed the Cross, with the Brazen Altar, the Brazen Laver, the Altar of Incense, and the Ark of the Covenant forming the upright posts, so to speak. The *"ephod"* was the outer robe worn by the high priests. It was made of two parts, one covering the back and the other the front, with these being joined together at the shoulders by golden clasps, which formed the setting for the onyx stones.

It contained all the colors used by the other material but with one addition, gold. Actually, this was more than a mere color, but rather gold wires, as portrayed in Verse 3, and were probably woven into the hem.

CUNNING WORK

"And they did beat the gold into thin plates, and cut it into wires, to work it in the blue, and in the purple, and in the scarlet, and in the fine linen, with cunning work.

"They made shoulderpieces for it, to couple it together: By the two edges was it coupled together" (Ex. 39:3-4).

This garment must have been strikingly beautiful! In fact, as we have just stated, these are the only garments in the history of man that were designed by the Lord of Glory, with

UPPER GARMENTS - THE EPHOD, THE CURIOUS GIRDLE , AND THE BREASTPLATE

the exception possibly of the skins provided for Adam and Eve by the Lord after the Fall.

Not only did the Lord design these garments for the priests, but, as well, He gave the workmen the cunning skill required to tailor each piece.

The colors in the garments represented not only who Christ was — God and King (gold and purple) — but, as well, the manner in which He would redeem humanity, i.e., the shedding of His blood (scarlet). The linen (white) represented His righteousness, while the blue emphasized the fact that all of this originated in Heaven.

THE CURIOUS GIRDLE

"And the curious girdle of his ephod that was upon it, was of the same, according to the work thereof; of gold, blue, and purple, and scarlet, and fine twined linen; as the Lord commanded Moses" (Ex. 39:5).

The *"curious girdle,"* one might say, was a sash tied around the waist. It was made of the same materials as was the ephod. It speaks of preparation for service.

THE NAMES OF THE CHILDREN OF ISRAEL

"And they wrought onyx stones enclosed in ouches of gold, graven as signets are graven, with the names of the Children of Israel.

"And he put them on the shoulders of the ephod, that they should be stones for a memorial to the Children of Israel; as the Lord commanded Moses" (Ex. 39:6-7).

These were shoulder boards, one might say, made of gold with two onyx stones, one on either side, with the names of the Children of Israel inscribed on these stones, six to each side.

As much as they were worn on the shoulders of the high priests, it tells us that these Twelve Tribes were, in effect, worn on the shoulders of Christ, with the shoulders denoting strength.

THE BREASTPLATE

"And he made the breastplate of cunning work, like the work of the ephod; of gold, blue, and purple, and scarlet, and fine twined linen.

"It was foursquare; they made the breastplate double: a span was the length thereof, and a span the breadth thereof, being doubled" (Ex. 39:8-9).

The *"breastplate,"* as is obvious, had the same colors as the ephod.

The Scripture doesn't tell us exactly how these colors were embroidered into these garments. Many scholars believe that the garments were all of white but around the borders, there was first of all a gold thread or wire, followed with a colored band of blue, and then of purple, and then of scarlet.

The breastplate being doubled probably pertained to the pouch, which contained the Urim and the Thummim.

THE URIM AND THE THUMMIM

"And you shall put in the breastplate of judgment the Urim and the Thummim; and they shall be upon Aaron's heart, when he goes in before the Lord: And Aaron shall bear the judgment of the Children of Israel upon his heart before the Lord continually" (Ex. 28:30).

It seems that in the back of the breastplate, there was a pocket of sorts right next to Aaron's heart, where was kept that referred to as the *"Urim and the Thummim."* The first word means *"lights,"* while the second means *"perfections."* So, we must conclude that the judgment rendered would be *"perfect."*

The Bible doesn't say exactly what these things were, but some believe they must have been material objects of some kind, possibly one stone with the word *"yes"* inscribed on it, and the second stone with the word *"no"* inscribed on it.

It seems that when a decision was to be made, the king, or whomever, would inquire of the high priest, who would give an answer by the Urim and the Thummim. The answer would be yes or no, according to the question asked.

As an example, it is said of David that he *"inquired of the LORD, saying, Shall I go and smite these Philistines? And the LORD said unto David, Go, and smite the Philistines, and save Keilah"* (I Sam. 23:2).

It seems that Abiathar had the ephod at this time, which contained the breastplate and, therefore, the Urim and the Thummim to which David inquired (I Sam. 22:20-23).

THE HOLY SPIRIT

Some may read these words and think as to how wonderful it would be presently to have something similar. Well, the truth is, what we have presently is a thousand times better. Due to the Cross, we now have the Holy Spirit in our hearts and lives, of whom these lights and perfections were but symbolic. Jesus said of the Divine Spirit, *"He will guide you into all truth: for He shall not speak of Himself; but whatsoever He shall hear, that shall He speak: and He will show you things to come"* (Jn. 16:13).

During the time of Israel, only a few had access to the high priest and, therefore, the Urim and the Thummim. Now, the most recently born-again saint has total, full, and complete access to the leading and guidance of the Holy Spirit, and on a continuing basis (Jn. 14:16). Our problem is, we take so little advantage of who the Holy Spirit is and what He can do for us. If anything at all, we mostly take Him for granted, meaning that we know so little about Him and how He works.

HOW THE HOLY SPIRIT WORKS

The Holy Spirit works entirely within the framework of the finished work of Christ, namely the Cross. This is what gives Him the legal authority to do all that He does. Paul said, *"The law of the Spirit of life in Christ Jesus, has made me free from the law of sin and death"* (Rom. 8:2).

Before the Cross, the Holy Spirit could not come into the hearts and lives of believers to abide permanently. The reason was that the blood of bulls and goats could not take away sins, meaning that the sin debt remained on all (Heb. 10:4). In other words, while animal blood was used as a stopgap measure, still, it was not sufficient within itself to take away sins. It could only cover sins, not take them away. That's the reason that John the Baptist said of Jesus when he introduced Him, *"Behold the Lamb of God who takes away the sin of the world"* (Jn. 1:29).

This had never been said before about any human being. Jesus was referred to as the Lamb of God simply because He was the fulfillment of all the millions of lambs that had been offered in the past. Now, *the* Lamb was present and would pay the price for the fallen sons of Adam's lost race.

Then John said that He, meaning Jesus, would take all of our sin away, not some of it, but all of it. This was something the blood of animals could not carry out.

So, when Jesus died on the Cross, this paid the debt in full for all who will believe, meaning that the Holy Spirit could now come into the hearts and lives of believers, there to abide forever (Jn. 14:16).

As well, before the Cross, when believers died, they could not be taken to Heaven, but rather were taken down into Paradise. They were actually captives of Satan. While the Evil One could not get them over into the burning side of the pit, they were definitely still his captives because the sin debt remained. Sin is what gives Satan the legal right to hold man captive. As stated, he could not hurt them, and, in reality they were comforted, but still, they were Satan's captives (Lk. 16:19-31). In fact, all of the Old Testament saints were in Paradise awaiting the Cross.

When Jesus died on the Cross, He went down into Paradise and *"led captivity captive,"* meaning that He made all of these people His captives, which meant they were no more captives of Satan. The Cross accomplished this.

Now when believers pass away, they instantly go to Heaven to be with the Lord Jesus Christ (Phil. 1:23). It is the Cross of Christ that made all of this possible.

Due to that fact, the Holy Spirit doesn't demand much of us, but He does demand one thing, and that is that our faith ever be anchored and maintained in Christ and what He did for us at the Cross. In other words, the Cross of Christ must be the object of our faith. When we speak of the Cross of Christ, we aren't speaking of the wooden beam on which He died, but rather what He there accomplished.

The story of the Bible is the story of *"Jesus Christ and Him Crucified."* So, when the believer places his or her faith exclusively in Christ and what Christ has done for us at the Cross, he, in effect, is placing his faith in the Word of God.

The believer must understand that every single thing that we receive from God, and I mean everything, all comes through Jesus Christ as the source and the Holy Spirit as the means, with the Cross of Christ making it all possible. That is the way the Holy Spirit works.

It is all by faith, but it must be faith in Christ and the Cross, that is, if God is to recognize such.

THE JEWELS ON THE BREASTPLATE

"And you shall set in it settings of stones, even four rows of stones: the first row shall be a sardius, a topaz, and a carbuncle: this shall be the first row.

"And the second row shall be an emerald, a sapphire, and a diamond.

"And the third row a ligure, an agate, and an amethyst.

"And the fourth row a beryl, and an onyx, and a jasper: they shall be set in gold in their enclosings.

"And the stones shall be with the names of the Children of Israel, twelve, according to their names, like the engravings of a signet: every one with his name shall they be according to the Twelve Tribes" (Ex. 28:17-21).

There were 12 jewels in number on the breastplate, one for each tribe, set in four rows of three each. As the names of the tribes of the Children of Israel were inscribed on the onyx stones on the shoulders of the high priest, signifying strength, likewise, the names were to be inscribed on the 12 stones worn over the heart of the high priest, signifying the love of God. So, this means that every single believer, for we are spiritual Israel, is secured by both strength and love. This strength and love is anchored in the Cross (Jn. 3:16).

Incidentally, it is virtually certain that all of these stones were the same size, which would have required an extraordinary skill of cutting as well as engraving, as it regarded the names being placed on each stone. As an aside, perhaps one could say without fear of contradiction that the Jews are the greatest diamond cutters, as well as cutters of other precious stones, in the world presently. Without a doubt, the great ability of this art began with the making of the breastplate.

THE RINGS OF GOLD AND THE CHAINS OF GOLD

"And you shall make upon the breastplate chains at the end of wreathen work of pure gold.

"And you shall make upon the breastplate two rings of gold, and shall put the two rings on the two ends of the breastplate.

"And you shall put the two wreathen chains of gold in the two rings which are on the ends of the breastplate.

"And the other two ends of the two wreathen chains you shall fasten in the two ouches, and put them on the shoulder pieces of the ephod before it.

"And you shall make two rings of gold, and shall put them upon the two ends of the breastplate in the border thereof, which is in the side of the ephod inward.

"And two other rings of gold you shall make, and shall put them on the two sides of the ephod underneath, toward the forepart thereof, over against the other coupling thereof, above the curious girdle of the ephod.

"And they shall bind the breastplate by the rings thereof unto the rings of the ephod with a lace of blue, that it may be above the curious girdle of the ephod, and that the breastplate be not loosed from the ephod.

"And Aaron shall bear the names of the Children of Israel in the breastplate of judgment upon his heart, when he goes in unto the Holy Place for a memorial before the Lord continually" (Ex. 28:22-29).

We find here that the breastplate was fastened by *"chains at the ends of wreathen work of pure gold,"* and these were passed through *"two rings of gold on the ends of the breastplate."* Thus, the people of God, as represented by their names, were chained to the high priest!

One could translate the beautiful artwork given here, as it relates to its spiritual meaning, to the words of Christ when He said: *"Take My yoke upon you, and learn of Me; for I am meek and lowly in heart: and you shall find rest unto your souls.*

"For My yoke is easy, and My burden is light" (Mat. 11:29-30).

The yoke, in a sense, is a harness or chain binding two or more objects together. We are bound to Christ, so much so, in fact, that He said of His own, *"I am the vine, you are the branches: he who abides in Me, and I in him, the same brings forth much fruit: for without Me you can do nothing"* (Jn. 15:5).

THE HEART

Once again, let us emphasize the fact that these precious stones were worn over the heart of the high priest, signifying the love of God for His people.

As a parent, or even a grandparent, we know somewhat, at least as far as a human being can know, of the love that God has for us. For our children, we want the best, and they are continually on our hearts. As well, we are continually on the heart of God, as He loves us with an undying love.

HOLY GARMENTS

"And you shall make holy garments for Aaron your brother for glory and for beauty" (Ex. 28:2).

The garments mentioned here are for Aaron the high priest. These garments were designed by the Lord, which were *"for glory and for beauty."* Aaron was a type of Christ, in fact, the greatest type at that particular time.

It is interesting to note that there were seven garments so designed, once again speaking of perfection.

They were:

1. The breastplate.
2. The ephod.
3. The robe.
4. The coat.
5. The mitre.
6. The girdle.
7. The plate of pure gold, which was fastened to the front of the mitre (headdress), and would have been positioned on his forehead, on which was engraved the words, *"Holiness to the Lord."*

FOR GLORY AND BEAUTY

The time of Alexander the Great was approximately 300 years before the time of Christ. It would have been approximately 1,200 years after the time of Moses.

Alexander formed the mighty Grecian Empire, laying mighty cities to waste in the process.

In his conquest of all of these cities, he now came to Jerusalem. He would do the same with it as he had done with the others, which was to issue a cryptic ultimatum, *"Surrender and live; rebel and die!"*

However, the night before the siege was to begin the next morning, he had a dream. He dreamed that he approached Jerusalem, and a man came out of the gates dressed in the most beautiful garments he had ever seen, pleading that the city be spared. The dream troubled him greatly, so much so that he accompanied his generals the next morning when they made their approach to Jerusalem.

Exactly as in his dream, the gate of the city opened, and a man came out dressed in garments that were beyond anything Alexander had ever seen. It was the great high priest of Israel. He pleaded for the city, and as he pleaded, the dream that Alexander had stood constantly before him. Fearful that he was insulting the *"gods,"* as he put it, he acceded to the requests and turned his army away from Jerusalem, thus, sparing the city.

However, the main point of these garments is that they represented Christ, even as we shall see.

THE SPIRIT OF WISDOM

"And you shall speak unto all who are wise hearted, whom I have filled with the spirit of wisdom, that they may make Aaron's garments to consecrate him, that he may minister unto Me in the priest's office" (Ex. 28:3).

The *"spirit of wisdom"* had to do with the Holy Spirit, who would enable the workers to properly make these garments that the Lord had designed. They must have been out of the ordinary for the spirit of wisdom to be needed.

As well, we must remember that this design was all of the Lord and none of Moses or any other man; consequently, it had to be adhered to minutely. Aaron could minister unto the Lord in the priest's office only as he followed the directions totally.

As we've already stated, our greatest problems in the church are that we seek to deviate from that which the Lord has given, desiring to institute our own design, etc. Of course, the Lord will have none of that.

MORE ABOUT THE ONYX STONES

These two onyx stones were a part of the ephod and were actually designed to join the back and the front of the ephod together at the shoulders. However, they were designed for more than merely holding the garment together.

These stones referred to as *"onyx"* were very different from the onyx of our times. Presently, it signifies a very ordinary stone, but the Hebrew word translated *"onyx"* here means *"to shine with the luster of fire."* Some argue that it was the *"beryl,"* with others claiming that it was the *"sardonyx."* More than likely it was the latter, being very expensive, if large, and these definitely were.

As stated, these two stones were on the shoulders of the high priests, with the front and the back of the ephod joined to them. On the stones were inscribed the names of the Twelve Tribes of the Children of Israel, six on one side and six on the other. They were to be inscribed according to the order of their birth.

The two large stones on the shoulders were set in plates of gold, held together by chains of gold.

Twice it states that this was done *"for a memorial."*

FOR A MEMORIAL

Concerning the Lord's Supper, twice He also said, *"This do in remembrance of Me"* (I Cor. 11:24-25).

While that which pertained to the high priest was before the fact, and that of the Lord's Supper after the fact, both speak of the Cross.

The shoulder speaks of security and strength, meaning that the Lord did carry Israel on His shoulders. He was able to do that because of the price that He would pay, guaranteeing redemption. Spiritually speaking, this holds true for us presently even more so than ever before. Concerning the lost sheep that was found, as Christ related the parable, He said, *"And when He has found it, He lays it on his shoulders, rejoicing"* (Lk. 15:5).

All of this signifies the strength of Christ and not at all our own personal strength. We are *"kept by the power of God"* (I Pet. 1:5). It is not our perseverance but His: *"He is able to keep that which I have committed unto Him"* (II Tim. 1:12).

In the words of Pink, he said, *"The shoulder which sustains the universe (Heb. 1:3), upholds the feeblest and most obscure member of the blood-bought congregation."*

Spiritually speaking, we are carried on the shoulders of Christ and not on the shoulders of anything else. Consequently, all believers who have separated their faith, partially believing in Christ and partially in something else, are in trouble, as would be obvious. Every other shoulder is feeble and unable to bear the load. Christ alone can take us through. When we say, *"Christ alone,"* we're speaking of what He did for us at the Cross. Our faith must rest in that and that alone!

THE ROBE

"And you shall make the robe of the ephod all of blue.

"And there shall be an hole in the top of it, in the midst thereof: it shall have a binding of woven work round about the hole of it, as it were the hole of a habergeon, that it be not rent" (Ex. 28:31-32).

Underneath the *"ephod"* and *"breastplate,"* the high priest was to wear a robe, or frock, wholly of blue. This robe was to have a hole for the head at the top, and it was to be woven without seam (Ex. 39:22). It was put on over the head like a coat of mail and probably reached below the knee.

The fact that it was *"all of blue"* offered a strong contrast to the other colors of the breastplate and ephod. It threw the portions of that attire into greater prominence.

The fact that it was all of blue tells us that it represented the ministry of Christ in Heaven, where He makes intercession for us, and does so by His very presence (Heb. 7:25-26).

THE GREAT DAY OF ATONEMENT

"And beneath upon the hem of it you shall make pomegranates of blue, and of purple, and of scarlet, round about the hem thereof; and bells of gold between them round about:

"A golden bell and a pomegranate, a golden bell and a pomegranate upon the hem of the robe round about.

"And it shall be upon Aaron to minister: and his sound shall be heard when he goes into the Holy Place before the LORD, and when he comes out, that he die not" (Ex. 28:33-35).

These passages speak of the high priest going into the Holy of Holies once a year on the Great Day of Atonement, actually going in three times. He first went in with incense to fill the Holy of Holies. The second time was to offer up blood on the Altar for himself because, even though he was the great high priest, he still was a sinful man. The third time was to take blood and put it on the Mercy Seat for the whole of Israel.

When he went into the Holy of Holies, he would divest himself of all the outer garments, including the robe of blue, leaving only the linen undergarments. This signified that Christ redeemed us, not with glory and beauty, but rather with His spotless righteousness, which was signified by His shed blood, symbolized by the white linen.

He would offer up blood on the Mercy Seat and then come back into the Holy Place, where he would then put on the blue robe.

THE POMEGRANATES AND THE BELLS

The pomegranates were probably made like tassels and had the colors of blue, purple, and scarlet. These colors signified the same as on the ephod, etc. These tassels went all the way around the robe of blue but were interspersed with *"bells of gold."* These were real bells, as would be obvious, and would ring whenever the high priest walked or moved. Of how many these were, the Scriptures are silent.

LOWER GARMENTS - THE POMEGRANATES AND THE BELLS

However, when the high priest came out of the Holy of Holies, once again putting on the blue robe, as would be obvious, the bells would begin to ring, which signified that He, of course, was alive, and that the blood of the sacrifice had been accepted.

As would be obvious, the pomegranates signified fruit. The Lord addressed this when He said, *"I am the vine, you are the branches: he who abides in Me and I in him, the same brings forth much fruit"* (Jn. 15:5).

The bells of gold represent the *"gifts of the Spirit"* (I Cor. 12:7-10).

All of this signifies that our Great High Priest, the Lord Jesus Christ, has shed His life's blood, thereby, making atonement, a sacrifice, which will never again have to be repeated. We know His sacrifice of Himself has been accepted by God because He has sent back the Holy Spirit with the fruit of the Spirit (pomegranates) and, as well, the gifts of the Spirit (the ringing of the bells). So, every time one begins to speak with other tongues, or else, gifts of the Spirit are manifested, one might say that this is the *"ringing of the bells."*

Israel knew that when the bells began to ring, the great high priest was soon to come out of the Holy Place. Likewise, we know now that the manifestation of the Holy Spirit proclaims the fact that our Great High Priest, the Lord Jesus Christ, is about to come back.

THE MITRE

The mitre was a type of headdress worn by the high priest.

The golden plate and its engraving pictured Israel as perfect before the Lord. As imperfect as Israel actually was within herself, as thus represented by Aaron and his crown, a type of Christ, she was holiness itself. The same is said for modern believers.

HOLINESS TO THE LORD

"And you shall make a plate of pure gold, and grave upon it, like the engravings of a signet, HOLINESS TO THE LORD" (Ex. 28:36).

This golden plate was the symbol of the essential holiness of the Lord Jesus. The saints are represented by Him and accepted in Him. Because of our legal and vital union with Him, His holiness is ours. So, what am I saying?

I am saying that you as a believer must look away from yourself, with your 10,000 failures, and put your eye on that golden plate, where it is inscribed, *"Holiness unto the Lord."* You can behold, in the perfections of your Great High Priest, the measure of your eternal acceptance with God. Christ is our sanctification as well as our righteousness!

THINGS THE BELIEVER MUST KNOW

Every true believer in the Lord is looked at by God as perfectly righteous, perfectly holy, perfectly pure, and perfectly Christlike! In fact, God can accept no less. However, we are all of this, not because of anything we have done, but simply and purely because of Christ. He is the altogether perfect One. Our salvation is in Him, just as our sanctification is in Him.

We are in Him by virtue of being baptized into His death and buried with Him by baptism into death. We are then raised with Him in *"newness of life"* (Rom. 6:3-4).

This is not speaking of water baptism, but rather of the crucifixion of Christ, His burial and resurrection, and our part in that threefold work.

Whenever you as a believing sinner registered faith in Christ, in the mind of God, you were literally *"in Christ"* when He died, was buried, and raised from the dead. As stated, your faith put you there!

FAITH

It's your faith that keeps you there, which refers to your sanctification. You were saved by faith, and you must understand that you are sanctified by faith as well! So, whatever you do, don't fall into the trap of being saved by faith and then trying to be sanctified by self.

Now, when we say *"faith,"* we are meaning that the Cross of Christ must ever be the object of your faith, and we speak of what Jesus there did.

This means that every single true believer on the face of the earth, in fact, all who have ever lived, are all looked at identically by the Lord. I speak of perfection, for God can accept no less!

We must know that I'm speaking of the way that God looks at us and the position we hold in Christ. The truth is, our *"condition"* is never up to our *"position,"* with the Holy Spirit constantly trying to pull the condition to where it ought to be. While we will never reach the place of perfection, we are definitely to reach the place that *"sin no longer has dominion over us"* (Rom. 6:14). Dominion is when the sin nature rules the individual, and that's a sad state of affairs, but yet, where virtually all Christians now find themselves. It is that simply because they do not understand God's prescribed order of victory, which is Christ and what Christ has done for us at the Cross.

WHAT IS THE DIFFERENCE IN THE CONSECRATED CHRISTIAN AND THE UNCONSECRATED CHRISTIAN?

The difference is twofold:

1. The consecrated enjoys the blessings of the Lord in many and varied ways. The unconsecrated Christian is under chastisement more often than not, which means that he is deprived of much of what the Lord would like to do for him but simply cannot because of obvious reasons. The one who walks close to the Lord enjoys benefits which are absolutely phenomenal, to say the least! He has the leading of the Spirit, the power of the Spirit, and, in fact, the help of the Spirit in every capacity. The unconsecrated Christian enjoys precious little of this.

Now, please understand that we're speaking here of true believers and not the millions who profess salvation, but actually have never been born again.

THE PLACE OF BLESSING

We must know that the place of blessing to which the consecrated Christian arrives is not because of anything great that we have done. In fact, as far as works are concerned, there is nothing that one can do that will garner one such a position and place in Christ. As previously stated, it is all done by faith, and I speak of faith in Christ and what Christ has done for us at the Cross.

2. When we all stand at the judgment seat of Christ where eternal rewards will be given, it should be obvious that the consecrated believer will receive eternal rewards far greater than the unconsecrated counterparts.

Paul said, *"There is one glory of the sun, and another glory of the moon, and another glory of the stars: for one star differs from another star in glory."*

He then said, *"So also is the resurrection of the dead"* (I Cor. 15:41-42).

This tells us that the *"glory,"* which speaks of rewards of every description, will be different with believers.

Considering that we're speaking of eternal consequences, we should understand how important all of this actually is.

Many Christians flippantly state that they will be happy just making Heaven, meaning that they couldn't care less about the rewards. Such thinking is foolish, to say the least!

WHAT IS HOLINESS?

Once again, holiness is not what we necessarily do but what we are because of what we believe. If we believe right, we will do right!

There is no way that a believer, irrespective as to what he might do, can make himself holy. It is not within our power to do such!

All of our holiness is 100 percent in Christ. If it is to be noticed, this golden plate, engraved with the words, *"Holi-*

ness to the Lord," was on the forehead of the high priest and not on anyone else. Actually, as previously stated, during his time, the high priest was the greatest example and type of Christ in the world of that day. This signified that the holiness is 100 percent in Christ.

Whenever the believer places his faith exclusively in Christ and what Christ has done for us at the Cross, that is holiness. The Holy Spirit can then work within our hearts and lives, making us what we ought to be. Regrettably, far too many believers count themselves as holy if they do certain things. Let us state it again: holiness is not attained by doing, but rather by believing, and more particularly, believing in the right thing, which is Christ and Him crucified. All holiness is in Christ. That means all of our holiness is because of Christ, and solely because of Christ and our faith in His finished work.

THE BLUE LACE

"And you shall put it on a blue lace, that it may be upon the mitre; upon the forefront of the mitre it shall be" (Ex. 28:37).

The *"blue lace"* once again signified Heaven. As we have stated, every single thing about the Tabernacle and its furnishings, as well as the attire of the priests, all and without exception had reference to Christ as it regarded His atoning, mediatorial, and intercessory work. That's the reason that we constantly say that believers ought to understand the Old Testament, and unless they understand it, they cannot really understand the New Testament.

In fact, the entirety of the Bible portrays Christ, but more particularly, it portrays Christ as it regards His sacrificial work. It is impossible to separate the Word of God from the Cross of Christ or the Cross of Christ from the Word of God. If you study the Bible at all, you will quickly come to see that everything in it, in one way or the other, portrays Christ and His Cross. When I speak of the Cross, I'm speaking of something that took place some 2,000 years ago, but which has continued benefits, in fact, benefits which will never be discontinued. It's the benefits of which we speak and certainly not a wooden beam!

The golden plate was to occupy a place of prominence on the front of the mitre or hat of the high priest. This certainly should signify the importance of the emphasis that God places on holiness.

THE FOREHEAD

"And it shall be upon Aaron's forehead, that Aaron may bear the iniquity of the holy things, which the Children of Israel shall hallow in all their holy gifts; and it shall be always upon his forehead, that they may be accepted before the LORD" (Ex. 28:38).

"Upon his heart before the Lord ... continually" (Ex. 28:29) and *"upon his forehead before the Lord continually,"* proclaim the fact that these statements united together reveal the untiring activity of the heart and mind of the Greater than Aaron on behalf of His people.

What does it mean, *"That Aaron may bear the iniquity of the holy things"*?

Imperfection attaches to everything that man does, and even the sacrifices that the people offered to God were required to be atoned for and purified. It was granted to the high priest in his official capacity to make the necessary atonement and so render the people's gifts acceptable.

Christ is now the mediator between God and men, and He alone is the mediator! (I Tim. 2:5; Heb. 8:6; 9:15; 12:24). As stated, God can accept nothing but that it is perfectly holy. Christ is perfectly holy, and our faith in Him grants us His perfect holiness as well. Then, whatever we do, and I speak of our efforts to live for the Lord, is *"accepted before the Lord."*

THE COAT, THE MITRE, AND THE GIRDLE

"And you shall embroider the coat of fine linen, and you shall make the mitre of fine linen, and you shall make the girdle of needlework" (Ex. 28:39).

Both Aaron's sons and he were to wear similar undergarments, but Aaron's vest was to be embroidered. We aren't told if the embroidery had colors or not, but probably not! The embroidery on Aaron's undergarment alone signified the following: the very fact of embroidery speaks of a finished work. The fact that the garments of Aaron's sons contained no embroidery tells us

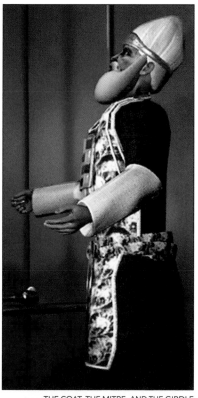

THE COAT, THE MITRE, AND THE GIRDLE

that their work was never finished, which, in fact, it wasn't. They were continually offering up sacrifices simply because the blood of bulls and goats could not really take away sins. However, Aaron, being the more particular type of Christ, specified what the work of Christ would be, which would be one sacrifice, once and for all, the sacrifice of Himself. The *"embroidery"* specified this.

As well, the *"fine linen"* of both the undergarment and the mitre, which was the hat or crown worn by Aaron, signified also the prefect righteousness of Christ.

The *"girdle of needlework"* spoke of service, and various different types of service, symbolized by the needlework.

FOR GLORY AND FOR BEAUTY

"And for Aaron's sons you shall make coats, and you shall make for them girdles and bonnets shall you make for them, for glory and for beauty" (Ex. 28:40).

The mention of *"Aaron's sons"* referred to his actual sons at the time and his descendants afterward, to whom the priesthood was rigidly confined.

It seems to imply that the attire of the priests, other than the high priest, was a dress of pure white without anything ornamental, such as the colors on Aaron's garments. Still, these snow-white garments, which, as stated, signified the righteousness of Christ, were still looked at as garments *"for glory and for beauty."* In fact, white robes have certainly a vast amount of scriptural testimony in their favor (Lev. 16:4; Mk. 9:3; Jn. 20:12; Acts 1:10; Rev. 4:4; 6:11; 7:9, 14, etc.).

As well, all of the priests, with the exception of Aaron the high priest, wore *"bonnets,"* which seem to have been close-fitting caps. These were not bonnets in the modern sense. They were probably shaped like a cup and did fit snugly on the head. They were totally different than the mitre worn by Aaron.

THE ANOINTING

"And you shall put them upon Aaron your brother, and his sons with him; and shall anoint them, and consecrate them, and sanctify them, that they may minister unto Me in the priest's office" (Ex. 28:41).

We are told here that the priests were to be anointed, consecrated, and set apart for the work of God exclusively; however, it remains unto Exodus, Chapter 29, for us to be told how all of this took place. It was, as we shall see, a very involved process.

But yet, everything that was done, the entirety of the ceremony, was only a representation in symbolic form of what Christ would do in reality.

That's the reason that Paul said: *"But now* (since the Cross) *has He obtained a more excellent ministry, by how much also He is the mediator of a better covenant, which was established upon better promises.*

"For if that first covenant had been faultless, then should no place have been sought for the second" (Heb. 8:6-7).

A COVERING

"And you shall make them linen breeches to cover their nakedness; from the loins even unto the thighs they shall reach" (Ex. 28:42).

The clothing covering the *"nakedness"* had as much, or more, to do with the judgment of God than it did modesty.

While it certainly included the latter, the greater meaning had to do with judgment upon sin.

When Adam fell, he told the Lord, *"I was afraid, because I was naked; and I hid myself"* (Gen. 3:10).

It is believed that Adam and Eve were covered by light before the Fall. Because of the Fall, the light was now gone, and they were very much aware now of their nakedness.

However, they were much more naked to the judgment of God than anything else. In a sense, clothing symbolizes the covering for sin, but we must remember, it is only a symbol. The immodesty in much of the modern dress, especially as it regards the female gender, in essence, is saying that they deny that they have sin and, consequently, do not need a covering. However, that's been man's problem all along!

He doesn't like to admit that he's a sinner, and even above that, he doesn't want to admit that it is only the shed blood of Jesus Christ that can cleanse from all sin (I Jn. 1:9).

DEATH

"And they shall be upon Aaron, and upon his sons, when they come in unto the Tabernacle of the congregation, or when they come near unto the altar to minister in the Holy Place; that they bear not iniquity and die: It shall be a statute forever unto him and his seed after him" (Ex. 28:43).

The Lord took this so seriously that the priests were warned that if they ignored any part of their garments, even those which were covered, such as the undergarments, they could be stricken that they die. In fact, two of Aaron's sons were stricken by God, but it was because of offering up *"strange fire"* (Lev. 10:1-2). Then the Lord added this further warning: *"It shall be a statute forever unto him and his seed after him."*

Many would claim that this no longer holds simply because it was all fulfilled in Christ.

In a sense, that is true; however, spiritually speaking, it continues to hold true and, in fact, must hold true. What do we mean by that?

All of these rules and ceremonies were given by the Lord for a particular purpose and reason. To be sure, He was dead serious about what He was doing. It involved the salvation of souls and was meant to portray Christ and His atoning work.

So, this question may be asked: If death visited those who took lightly the symbol, how much more, spiritually speaking, will it visit those who insult the reality?

To ignore, add to, or take from the finished work of Christ in any way demands the judgment of God. It cannot be otherwise! It even pertains to believers.

While the Lord doesn't require perfection, at least of our own efforts, He definitely does require faith, but faith in the proper object, and we continue to speak of Christ and Him crucified.

> *"When they crucified my Saviour on the Cross of Calvary,*
> *"There a blessed fount was opened*
> *"For my cleansing full and free,*
> *"And my sins were all forgiven,*
> *"Just by faith in His shed blood,*
> *"They are washed away forever*
> *"By the crimson flood."*

14
Strange Fire

CHAPTER FOURTEEN

Strange Fire

"AND NADAB AND *Abihu, the sons of Aaron, took either of them his censer, and put fire therein, and put incense thereon, and offered strange fire before the LORD, which He commanded them not.*

"*And there went out fire from the LORD, and devoured them, and they died before the LORD*" (Lev. 10:1-2).

It may seem somewhat strange closing this book with this chapter concerning the death of two priests. However, I think it is fitting in that the Holy Spirit would show us how important all of this is. Please understand, if such judgment was given by the Lord against two of His priests, as it regarded a defilement of the symbolism, how much more is judgment on that which is a biblical reality!

Chapter 9 of Leviticus closes with fire coming out from the Lord, who dwelt between the Mercy Seat and the Cherubim in the Holy of Holies. The fire consumed the sacrifice on the Brazen Altar, which was a display of the glory of God, which greatly benefited the people (Lev. 9:4, 6, 23-24). But now, the same fire came from the Lord from the same place (the Holy of Holies) but rather killed two of the priests, Nadab and Abihu, sons of Aaron. The first fire was glory; the second was judgment, although the same fire. A powerful lesson, one of the greatest in the Bible, is to be learned here.

What was this *"strange fire"*?

Twice a day, at the time of the morning and evening sacrifices (9 a.m. and 3 p.m.), the priests were to burn holy incense before the Lord, and it was to be done in the following manner.

THE WAY OF THE LORD

They were to take coals of fire from the Brazen Altar, and only from the Brazen Altar, and put those coals of fire on the Golden Altar (the Altar of Incense), which sat immediately in front of the Veil, which hid the Holy of Holies, where God dwelt between the Mercy Seat and the Cherubim.

Incense was to be poured over these coals of fire, which would fill the Holy Place.

As stated, this fire had to come from the Brazen Altar, which was a type of Christ and His great sacrifice of Himself on the Cross of Calvary. This is what the Brazen Altar typified, making it important beyond our comprehension.

So, the fire that Nadab and Abihu used didn't come from this source but, more than likely, from one of the fires which had been made for boiling the sacrificial flesh. That being the case, it definitely would have been fire used for spiritual purposes, but it was not fire from the Brazen Altar.

The idea is, it doesn't really matter from where the fire came, from whatever ignition, if it's not from the Brazen Altar, it could not be accepted. It is the same presently, and even more so, considering that the Brazen Altar was but a symbol.

THE BRAZEN ALTAR — A TYPE OF CALVARY

As stated, the coals of fire, which were to be placed on the Golden Altar, had to come from the Brazen Altar (Lev. 16:12). God would accept no other, and as I think is overly obvious, looked at the presentation of other fire as a most grave offense, which brought death to two priests.

I think one can say without fear of contradiction that the Brazen Altar was the crowning vessel of all the sacred vessels. One may think that the Ark of the Covenant, covered by the Mercy Seat, over which looked the Cherubim, was the crowning piece. While that definitely was the place where God dwelt, which typified His throne, the idea is that august place could not be reached until it was reached by way of the Brazen Altar. The Brazen Altar, typifying Calvary, was the key to all things. The sacrifices were offered on this altar, and this altar alone.

FORBIDDEN

In fact, God absolutely forbid sacrifices to be offered on the Golden Altar. The blood alone could be applied to or sprinkled on the horns of the Golden Altar, but sacrifices, strange incense, meat offerings, or any drink offering must not be offered or poured thereon (Ex. 30:9). In other words, to do such was, in effect, to bypass Calvary, which God could not tolerate. Man can come before God only on one premise, and that is by and through the shed blood of the Lord Jesus Christ. That, and that alone, which the Brazen Altar and its sacrifices typified, gains entrance to God in any form. When Jesus said, *"No man comes unto the Father but by Me,"* He was speaking of what He would do at the Cross of Calvary, which would make all of this possible (Jn. 14:6).

Nadab and Abihu were priests of God, which means they were ordained of God, called of God, and anointed by God. Whenever they ignored the Cross, which is actually what they did, the results of judgment were immediate. It is no less presently!

Let me say it again, all of the vessels in the Tabernacle, including the Brazen Altar, were mere symbols of the reality. So, if God was this serious about the symbols, don't you think that the reality is much more serious?

THE SIN OF THE MODERN CHURCH

Regarding most of the modern church, the Cross has been ignored, set aside, and even repudiated in some cases. In fact, the modern church is a Crossless church, which worships a Crossless Christ. As such, it worships *"another Jesus"* (II Cor. 11:4), that is, if it worships at all!

Most of the worship is *"will worship,"* of which we will have more to say momentarily, which means that it is worship that does not originate at the Cross.

All false doctrine in some way has its origination in a false interpretation of the Cross. Paul said: *"For many walk, of whom I have told you often, and now tell you even weeping, that they are the enemies of the Cross of Christ:*

"Whose end is destruction, whose god is their belly, and whose glory is in their shame, who mind earthly things" (Phil. 3:18-19).

The Message of the Cross, in reality, is the foundation of all Bible doctrine. Within itself, even though it may be referred to as a doctrine, it is not merely a doctrine, but rather the foundation on which all doctrine is built, at least if it's true biblical doctrine. I am absolutely positive that Jesus looked at the sacrificial offering of Himself on the Cross of Calvary as more than a mere doctrine. No! While everything that Jesus did was of utmost significance, still, while the correct terminology regarding the Cross could be referred to as a doctrine, it is actually the foundation on which all biblical doctrine is built.

In fact, the doctrine of the Cross was formulated in the mind of the Godhead from before the foundation of the world. As far as we know, it is the first doctrine, hence, it being the foundation of all doctrine (I Pet. 1:18-20).

If the Cross is not the foundation of all doctrine, then, in some way, that which is presented is strange fire.

FIRE

Let the reader understand that it definitely was fire that Nadab and Abihu offered. It looked just like the fire from the Brazen Altar. However, even though it looked like that fire and, in fact, by mere observation, could not be distinguished from that fire, God knew it was strange fire and acted accordingly.

All types of strange fire are being offered up today in Christendom. They look right, and they look real in some cases, but they do not originate with the Cross. As a result, they cannot be right, and most definitely, they will ultimately be judged by God.

Rather than trying to name the types of strange fire, suffice to say, anything that ignores the Cross, registers unbelief toward the Cross, or repudiates the Cross is strange fire, irrespective of how good it may look on the surface.

We believe that the Word of God teaches that when Jesus died on the Cross, He addressed Himself to every single problem facing the human race, in other words, everything that was lost at the Fall. While it is true that in the atonement, there are some things, such as the glorified body, which we will not have until the coming resurrection, but, still, everything was addressed. Not only did Paul say so, but Peter did as well (II Pet. 1:3-4). When it comes to sin, no matter what the bondage might be or whatever the sin might be, whether it's judged to be little or large, Jesus answered it at the Cross. There He defeated Satan, along with every single demon spirit and fallen angel. He did it by atoning for all sin, past, present, and future (Col. 2:10-15). So, if the preacher is not preaching the Cross, then he's not preaching the Gospel. He might be preaching about the Gospel and, as such, say some good things, but until he preaches the Cross, he's not preaching the Gospel (I Cor. 1:17-18, 21, 23; 2:2).

Paul said, *"For after that in the wisdom of God the world by wisdom knew not God, it pleased God by the foolishness of preaching* (preaching the Cross) *to save them who believe"* (I Cor. 1:21).

PREACHING THE CROSS

The Holy Spirit through Paul is not claiming here that preaching is foolishness or that preaching the Cross is foolishness, but that this is the way the world looks at the situation.

He also said, *"For the preaching of the Cross is to them who perish foolishness; but unto us which are saved it is the power of God"* (I Cor. 1:18).

Therefore, this means that the foray of the church into humanistic psychology is a slap in the face of Christ, in effect, a repudiation of the Cross. This states, whether admitted or not, that the Cross is insufficient and that worldly wisdom is needed as well. What a travesty and what stupidity! What an abomination! That's at least one of the reasons that Jesus said, *"You are they which justify yourselves before men; but God knows your hearts: for that which is highly esteemed among men is abomination in the sight of God"* (Lk. 16:15).

THE CROSS OF CHRIST IS THE DIVIDING LINE

As should be plainly and clearly obvious, the Cross is not something that can be ignored. Anyone, even as we have previously stated, who honestly reads the Bible, cannot help but see the Cross as the central theme of the entirety of the Word of God. Once again, as we've already said a number of times, at this present time, the Holy Spirit is making the Cross so visible that it can no longer be ignored. One will either have to accept it or reject it. In other words, there will be no neutral Christians as it regards the Cross of Christ.

Those who reject the Cross, ignore the Cross, or even try to link it with something else are going to be placed on the side of the apostate church. There is no place else to be as it regards this particular position. Those who embrace the Cross will be in the true church.

In fact, this is the way that it has always been. The Cross has ever been the dividing line, and so this is not something new. However, I personally feel that the emphasis that the Holy Spirit is now placing on the Cross, one might say, is new. These are the last of the last days, and the world is saddled with a church that says, *"I am rich, and increased with goods, and have need of nothing."* However, Christ says, *"And knowest not that you are wretched, and miserable, and poor, and blind, and naked"* (Rev. 3:17).

THAT FOR WHICH GOD HAS CALLED US

I personally feel, as well, that the Lord has raised up this particular ministry (Jimmy Swaggart Ministries) to take this Message of the Cross to the world. He is giving us the means to do so through television. In fact, at this particular time (April 2014), we are now airing television over about one-half of the world.

We believe the Lord has commissioned us to place the television programming in every city in the world that will accept it, and that, by the grace of God, is what we are doing. Even as I dictate these notes, we will go on tomorrow in the great country of Italy, airing 24 hours a day, seven days a week, in 4.7 million homes. In fact, we could name scores of countries of the world in the same manner.

Of all the things the Lord has helped us to do and helped us to see in past years, I do believe that this which He is presently doing will help us to have a greater impact on the church than ever before. In fact, I believe we're going to see the greatest number of people saved that we have ever seen in the history of this ministry and, as well, hundreds of thousands baptized with the Holy Spirit with the evidence of speaking with other tongues. In fact, I think this is the very reason, or at least one of the primary reasons, the Lord has given to me the revelation of the Cross. It is not for me only, as should be obvious, but it is for the entirety of the Body of Christ.

WILL WORSHIP

Acceptable worship can only be in the energy of the Holy Spirit, in the truth of the shed blood of Jesus Christ, and in obedience to the inspired Word. The fire of the Holy Spirit associates itself alone with the blood of the crucified Saviour. Now, the believer must understand this, and must understand it perfectly, because we are speaking here of the fate of the eternal soul. One must know that all other fire is strange fire.

Mackintosh said, *"Of necessity, the Lord must pour out His righteous judgment upon all false worship, though He will never 'quench the smoking flax nor break the bruised reed.' The thought of this is most solemnizing, when one calls to mind the thousands of censers, so to speak, smoking with strange fire throughout the wide domain of modern Christendom."*

WORSHIP

Everyone who knows, through grace, the pardon of his sins through the atoning blood of Jesus can worship the Father in spirit and in truth. To be sure, these things can only be known in a divine way. They do not belong to the flesh or to nature. In fact, they do not even belong to this earth. They are spiritual and they are heavenly.

Sadly, very much, if not most, of that which passes among men for the worship of God is but strange fire. It is fire that has been brought from man's own ingenuity, strength, and ability. In other words, no matter how good it looks and no matter that it is real fire, if it did not come from the Brazen

Altar, which means that it did not come from the Cross, it cannot be accepted by God.

However, let it be readily known that rejection by God at the same time demands judgment.

JUDGMENT

The Lord is patient with all of us, and we thank God for that a thousand times over. Where would any of us be if His patience were not as it is?

However, whenever the time comes that the *"light"* is shown in all of its full glory, if that light is rejected, judgment is swift and sure, just as it was with Nadab and Abihu. So, what am I saying?

I'm saying that the Holy Spirit is now making the Message of the Cross clear and plain to the entirety of the church. They're going to have to make a choice. With many, it will mean giving up their respective churches, even their respective denominations. With many, it will mean giving up their circle of friends and even their family. However, if we stop and think a moment, that's exactly what Jesus demanded.

He plainly said: *"If any man will come after Me, let him deny himself and take up his cross daily, and follow Me.*

"For whosoever will save his life shall lose it: But whosoever will lose his life for My sake, the same shall save it" (Lk. 9:23-24).

The fire of judgment will consume the sacrifice, i.e., "Christ," or else, it will consume the individual. In other words, we go the way of Christ, which is the Cross, or we face the judgment of God.

I WILL BE SANCTIFIED IN
THEM WHO COME NEAR ME

"Then Moses said unto Aaron, This is it that the LORD spoke, saying, I will be sanctified in them who come near Me, and before all the people I will be glorified. And Aaron held his peace.

"And Moses called Mishael and Elzaphan, the sons of Uzziel, the uncle of Aaron, and said unto them, Come near, and carry your brethren from before the sanctuary out of the camp.

"So they went near, and carried them in their coats out of the camp; as Moses had said" (Lev. 10:3-5).

Quite possibly, Moses inquired of the Lord as to why Nadab and Abihu were stricken dead. The answer was straightforward: *"I will be sanctified in them who come near Me, and before all the people I will be glorified."*

The Lord is saying by this statement that if men place on His altar the workings of their own corrupt will, what must be the result? Judgment! Sooner or later, judgment must come! It may linger, but it will come. It cannot be otherwise.

What did the Lord mean by the statement, *"I will be sanctified in them who come near Me, and before all the people I will be glorified?"*

GOD'S WAY

In essence, He was meaning that things will be done His way, or judgment will come. *"To be sanctified"* means *"to be set apart."* In this instance, it means *"to be set apart to God's way."*

What is that way?

I think it is overly obvious as to what that way is, as presented here in Chapter 10 of Leviticus.

His way is, *Jesus Christ and Him crucified* (I Cor. 1:23). If another way is instituted by man, it is a way that is abominable to God, irrespective as to how religious it may seem to be on the surface.

To be sure, Cain did not refuse to offer a sacrifice. In fact, he offered a beautiful sacrifice, but it just happened to be a sacrifice that God could not accept. It was the labor of Cain's own hands, which means that it was polluted to begin with.

There is only one sacrifice that God will recognize, and that is the sacrifice of Christ. When we recognize that sacrifice, place all of our faith and hope in that sacrifice, we are then sanctifying God. When we fail to do so, God will not fail to be sanctified. He will pour out judgment upon that which rebels against Him, which, as well, sanctifies Him.

We must understand that salvation in every capacity is all of God and none of man. This means if man tries to change God's way by inserting his own way into the effort, God cannot condone it or accept it in any way. That is the sin of mankind in general.

LEST YOU DIE

"*And Moses said unto Aaron and unto Eleazar, and unto Ithamar, his sons, Uncover not your heads, neither rend your clothes; lest you die, and lest wrath come upon all the people: but let your brethren, the whole house of Israel, bewail the burning which the Lord has kindled.*

"And you shall not go out from the door of the Taberna-cle of the congregation, lest you die: for the anointing oil of the Lord is upon you. And they did according to the word of Moses" (Lev. 10:6-7).

We find here that Aaron, his other two sons, Eleazar and Ithamar, as well as the entirety of the nation of Israel, were now in great danger of the wrath of God being poured out upon them as well.

Why was this so?

While it would have been proper for the people of Israel to have mourned the deaths of these priests, the high priest and his remaining sons must prove their submission to the divine chastisement by crushing their individual feelings of sorrow. In fact, a murmur on their part would have brought God's wrath on themselves, and even on Israel as a whole, whom they represented.

THE CROSS

These priests could not stop their duties for one moment, even for the sake of burying their dead. Others would have to perform this task.

For the priests to have mourned would, in essence, have been saying that the Cross was of little significance. Regrettably, that's what many modern preachers are now saying.

They pray, or at least what little they do pray, with no thought of the Cross. They worship, if you could call it worship, but it is rather that which God does not recognize as worship simply because they attempt to approach God without the benefit of the shed blood of the Lamb. They send needy souls to humanistic psychologists, which means that they are expressing a vote of no confidence as it regards the Cross.

The truth is, with many of these preachers, neither they nor the people they lead are saved, but for those who definitely are saved, and some definitely are, chastisement is about to follow. If that is rejected, judgment will follow, and it will not be a pretty picture.

The Lord plainly told the priests through Moses, *"You will do as I say, or you will die!"* Is it any different now?

THE DAY OF GRACE

Many think that because this is the dispensation of grace, and it definitely is, God withholds all judgment. Nothing could be further from the truth. The facts are, God makes greater demands now, and I speak of this dispensation of grace, even than He did under Law.

Listen again to Paul, **"And the times of this ignorance** *(before the Cross)*, **God winked at; but now** *(this Day of Grace)* **commands all men everywhere to repent"** **(Acts 17:30).**

Under grace, which has been brought about by the Cross, much more light is given to a darkened world; consequently, much more is expected, once again, as should be obvious!

The judgment of God presently may not be as obvious and as pointed as it was with these two priests; however, I greatly suspect that if the truth be known, many things which presently happen to individuals is actually the judgment of God. Although thought of as being for certain causes and reasons, and we speak of believers, or at least those who profess, what is taking place is very likely God's judgment being poured out.

THE NATURE OF GOD

We must never take lightly the divine nature of God. For those who stray, chastisement will come. If that fails, judgment will follow.

While God is love, His nature will never allow His righteousness to be impugned. In fact, He cannot allow such to happen. If He did, the entire structure of righteousness would collapse. He who loves must at the same time judge. If He doesn't, then it's not really love that's being shown. This means that the judgment of God is also the love of God.

Man can only be saved in one way, and that is by faith in the slain Lamb (Jn. 3:16; Rom. 5:8; Rev. 5:6).

STRONG DRINK

"And the Lord spoke unto Aaron, saying, 'Do not drink wine nor strong drink, you, nor your sons with you, when you go into the Tabernacle of the congregation, lest you die: it shall be a statute forever throughout your generations:

"And that you may put difference between holy and unholy, and between unclean and clean" (Lev. 10:8-10).

The Law as given by the Lord at this juncture indicates that Nadab and Abihu had acted under the excitement of intoxicating drink. In other words, they were drunk.

Some have claimed from these passages that it's satisfactory to drink in moderation, providing it's done at the right time, the right place, etc.

That's not what the Scripture is saying here.

In fact, this is a prohibition against strong drink in any capacity. The Lord was telling these priests, and all priests who would follow thereafter, that if they partook of strong drink regarding their duties in the Tabernacle or Temple, with the latter yet to come, they would run the risk of being stricken dead.

While they might not be stricken dead if they partook of strong drink outside of the Tabernacle, they would most definitely be courting disaster if they did so within the confines of the Tabernacle or its courts.

In no way do these passages make allowance for social drinking.

SOCIAL DRINKING

I believe the Bible teaches total and complete abstinence from all alcoholic beverages of any kind and at all times. Considering the heartache and sorrow that alcohol has caused, I cannot even remotely see how any Christian, striving to be a good example, would think it satisfactory to partake of alcohol in any capacity. Concerning most crimes committed, it is a known fact that the individual committing the crimes is under the influence of alcohol. While there are thousands of evil things that could be said about strong drink, there isn't one good thing, of which I am aware, that can be said. Let's briefly look at some of the instances in the Bible, which some have claimed gives license to moderate drinking, etc.

DID THE SAVIOUR USE INTOXICATING WINE IN THE LORD'S SUPPER?

No!

In the description of the Lord's Supper, the Bible never uses the word *"wine."* We are told, *"He took the cup, and gave thanks, and gave it to them, saying, Drink ye all of it"* (Mat. 26:27). Mark says, *"He took the cup, when He had given thanks, He gave it to them"* (Mk. 14:23). Luke says, *"He took the cup, and gave thanks, and said, Take this, and divide it among yourselves"* (Lk. 22:17). Jesus called this drink the *"fruit of the vine"* (Mat. 26:29; Mk. 14:25; Lk. 22:18). It seems the Holy Spirit carried this directive right on through, even into the Early Church. The Apostle Paul said, *"After the same manner also He took the cup, when He had supped, saying, This cup is the New Testament in My blood"* (I Cor. 11:25). Then, following, He mentioned *"this cup"* and then later on, *"that cup."* When these passages are read consecutively, it becomes clear that God intended for us to use grape juice in taking the Lord's Supper. I also think the Holy Spirit took particular pains not to use any words that could be construed as referring to any kind of intoxicating beverage. There is not a single reference in the Word of God that a person should use intoxicating wine for the Lord's Supper.

THE SYMBOL OF DECAY

The very meaning of fermented wine makes it unsatisfactory to represent the blood of the Lord Jesus Christ, which the juice taken in the Lord's Supper is definitely to represent.

Fermented wine is grape juice in which decay (or rot) has taken place. In other words, the process of fermentation is the breakdown of large molecules caused by the influence of bacteria or fungi. Wine, then, results from the degenerative action of germs on pure substances.

Fermented wine used in Communion would actually symbolize tainted, sinful blood, and not the pure and perfect blood of Jesus Christ that had to be made evident to be a perfect cleansing for our sins. Pure, fresh grape juice tends toward life, but fermented wine tends toward death. Alcohol used for drinking purposes is both a narcotic and a poison. It could hardly be used as a symbol for the blood of the Lord Jesus Christ.

LEAVEN

The Jews were required to use unleavened bread with the Passover Feast, and they were commanded that during that time, *"There shall no leavened bread be seen with you, neither shall there be leaven seen with you in all your quarters"* (Ex. 13:7). In other words, there was not even to be any leaven in the house.

As early as this, bread that had been tainted with bacteria or yeast, which comprises leaven, was considered unsuitable at the spiritual events celebrated by the Jews. Jesus also used unleavened bread in initiating the Lord's Supper. However, the New Testament makes no special issue of unleavened bread because this particular type of bread was a type of the perfection of the Lord Jesus Christ, which He fulfilled in totality in His personal life, making the symbol unnecessary anymore.

Consequently, the point that I make is this: if the Lord specifically chose bread that had no bacteria and no fungus spores in it to picture His broken body, do you honestly think He would choose alcoholic wine, fermented wine, which is directly the product of fungi or bacteria, to represent His blood? I hardly think so! The pure blood of Jesus Christ, as stated, is best represented by pure grape juice.

THE MORAL STATUTES

In the passage of our study, in addressing the high priests, along with all other priests under the old economy, the Lord commanded of them, *"Do not drink wine nor strong drink ... when you go into the Tabernacle of the congregation, lest you die: it shall be a statute forever throughout your generations."*
You must remember, these priests entering into the Tabernacle were types of the Lord Jesus Christ, who is our Great High Priest. Now I ask you a question: would Jesus, the night He was betrayed, drink intoxicating wine before going to the Crucifixion and entering into His high priestly work? I think not! It would have been a rejection and a contradiction of His own word, which we are now studying in Chapter 10 of Leviticus.
We must always remember that the word *"wine,"* as used in the Bible, simply means, *"the fruit of the vine."* It can mean either unfermented grape juice or intoxicating wine. So, when the word is read, whether it is New Testament or Old Testament, this distinction must always be kept in mind.
No, the beverage that Jesus used at the Lord's Supper was not intoxicating wine, and neither is it proper or permissible for us to use intoxicating wine in the Lord's Supper presently, or any other time for that matter.

THE WATER THAT JESUS TURNED TO WINE

Again, the answer is *"No!"* The water that Jesus turned to wine in John, Chapter 2, was not intoxicating wine. If it were so, our Lord was automatically placed in the position of providing men, who had already *"well drunk"* (Jn. 2:10), with more wine. If it was wine as we think of wine today, which is an intoxicating beverage, the Lord then would have been breaking His own law against temperance. The total amount of water turned into wine was about 150 gallons. If this had been an intoxicating beverage, it would have served as an invitation to drink and would have placed our Lord in the unsavory position of providing a flood of intoxicants for the people who had already consumed a considerable amount.

GOOD WINE

The word *"good"* was used to describe what the Lord had miraculously brought about. It is the Greek word *"kalos"* and is defined in Vine's Expository Dictionary of New Testament Words as denoting what is intrinsically good. Now, the pure, sweet juice of the grape could rightly be denoted as "intrinsically good"; but the rotted, fermented, decayed, spoiled, and intoxicating kind of wine could hardly be called good. It is easy to think of the term *"good"* in describing whatever the Lord makes. For example, in describing the Creation, Moses said, *"And God saw everything that He had made, and behold, it was very good"* (Gen. 1:31).

It is unthinkable that our Lord would have made corrupted, fermented wine at Cana and called it good. You see, fermentation is a kind of decomposition, just as are putrefaction and decay. It would be almost blasphemous to call that good in connection with our Lord.

Pliny, an ancient Greek scholar, said that *"good wine"* was a term used to denote the juice destitute of spirit. Albert Barnes said, *"The wine referred to here was doubtless such as was commonly drunk in Palestine."* That was the pure juice of the grape. It was not branded or drugged wine, and neither was it wine compounded of various substance, such as people drink in this land. The common wine of that day, which was drunk in Palestine, was the simple juice of the grape.

BLASPHEMY?

As well, it is tantamount to blasphemy, in my opinion, to suppose that the first miracle that Christ performed after being filled with the Holy Spirit (compare Mk. 1:9-12; Lk. 4:1) was an act of creating intoxicating wine for a crowd of celebrants, the kind of wine that would make them drunk. It is unthinkable!

Still another fact from the record in John, Chapter 2, is this: those men who had already drunk a considerable amount praised the bridegroom for having kept the *"good wine"* until the last. Now, it is a simple fact that alcohol drunk to any excess will deaden the taste buds of the drinker. If the wine in Cana of Galilee that the guests had already been partaking of was intoxicating wine (and they had already partaken of quite a bit at this point), then when the wine that Jesus had miraculously made was given to them, they could not have detected its taste. Their taste buds would have been deadened. To be honest with you, they would have been drunk by this time, or almost so. Only if they had been drinking the form of the vine's fruit that we know as grape juice, and then had been provided some fresh grape juice, would the governor of the feast have been able to make the observation he did.

WINE IN BIBLICAL TIMES

Even though there are several words in the Bible that denote wine, there are two words which are used more than any other. In the New Testament, it is the Greek word *"oinos,"* which can mean either fermented or unfermented wine.

Dr. Ferrar Fenton, a biblical translator, (the Holy Bible in Modern English), lists six different meanings of the word oinos:

1. Grapes, as fresh fruit
2. Raisins
3. Thick grape syrup
4. A thick jam
5. Fresh grape juice
6. Fermented grape juice

The last type would make you drunk.

Dr. Lyman Abbott said that fermented wine in Bible times was the least common of all wines. Even in the fermented kind, the percentage of alcohol was small.

In the Old Testament, the most often used Hebrew word for wine is *"yayin."* That word is found 141 times in the Old Testament and is used interchangeably, depending on the context.

Also, it is unthinkable that the Lord would have broken His own word: *"Wine is a mocker, strong drink is raging: and whosoever is deceived thereby is not wise ... Who has woe? Who has sorrow? Who has contentions? Who has babbling? Who has wounds without cause? Who has redness of eyes? They who tarry long at the wine; they who go to seek mixed wine. Do not look upon the wine when it is red, when it gives his colour in the cup, when it moves itself aright. At the last it bites like a serpent, and stings like an adder"* (Prov. 20:1; 23:29-32).

The reasons given above are sufficient proof that Jesus did not change water to the kind of wine that would make one drunk. Instead, it was a pure, sweet grape juice.

PROHIBITION

Before Prohibition, wine was considered to be exactly as it was in Bible times. However, when Prohibition was enacted in 1920, the term had to be defined more closely. Consequently, *"wine"* was designated to mean something that would make one drunk. The other kind of non-intoxicating beverage was called by whatever name desired, grape juice or whatever. Consequently, many people today confuse the simple word *"wine,"* as it was used in the Bible, with our understanding of that word presently, but that is not universally true.

No, Jesus' first miracle was not the making of wine that would make a person drunk. It was pure, fresh, sweet grape juice, and I believe that scripturally, scientifically, and legally we have proven that.

THE HOLY AND THE UNHOLY

As it was then, there is presently that which is holy and that which is unholy, and that which is clean and that which is unclean. Alcohol falls into the category of the unholy and the unclean, as ought to be overly obvious.

As well, there are many things presently in the world that are unholy and unclean with which a believer should not associate himself.

These things would consist of that which would be of harm to the physical body, which is the temple of the Holy

Spirit. This is at least one of the reasons that Paul said: *"And be not drunk with wine, wherein is excess; but be filled with the Spirit;*

"Speaking to yourselves in psalms, and hymns, and spiritual songs, singing and making melody in your heart to the Lord" (Eph. 5:18-19).

The idea is that believers be drunk with the Spirit instead of spirits.

> *"There have been names that I have loved to hear,*
> *"But never has there been a name so dear*
> *"To this heart of mine, as the name divine,*
> *"The precious, precious name of Jesus."*

> *"There is no name in earth or heaven above,*
> *"That we should give such honor and such love,*
> *"As the blessed name, let us all acclaim,*
> *"That wondrous, glorious name of Jesus."*

> *"And someday I shall see Him face to face,*
> *"To thank and praise Him for His wondrous grace,*
> *"Which He gave to me when He made me free,*
> *"The blessed Son of God called Jesus."*

Bibliography

CHAPTER 1

Arthur W. Pink, *Gleanings in Exodus*, Sovereign Grace
Publishers, Lafayette, 2002, pg. 180.

Ibid.

CHAPTER 2

Arthur W. Pink, *Gleanings in Exodus*, Sovereign Grace
Publishers, Lafayette, 2002, pg. 186.

Ibid., pg. 187.

Ibid., pg. 218.

CHAPTER 4

Arthur W. Pink, *Gleanings in Exodus*, Sovereign Grace
Publishers, Lafayette, 2002, pg. 232.

Jimmy Swaggart, *Jimmy Swaggart Bible Commentary:
Exodus*, World Evangelism Press, Baton Rouge, 2004.

Arthur W. Pink, *Gleanings in Exodus*, Sovereign Grace
Publishers, Lafayette, 2002, pg. 241.

CHAPTER 5

Arthur W. Pink, *Gleanings in Exodus*, Sovereign Grace Publishers, Lafayette, 2002, pg. 244.

Ibid., pg. 245.

CHAPTER 7

Arthur W. Pink, *Gleanings in Exodus*, Sovereign Grace Publishers, Lafayette, 2002, pg. 207.

Ibid., pg. 210.

C.J. Ellicott, *An Old Testament Commentary for English Readers by Various Writers*, Cassel, Petter, Galpin & Co., New York, 1882, pg. 450.

CHAPTER 8

H.D.M. Spence, *The Pulpit Commentary: Exodus 30:35*, Grand Rapids, Eerdmans Publishing Company, 1978.

George Williams, *William's Complete Bible Commentary*, Grand Rapids, Kregel Publications, 1994, pg. 60.

Arthur W. Pink, *Gleanings in Exodus*, Sovereign Grace Publishers, Lafayette, 2002, pg. 287.

CHAPTER 10

George Williams, *William's Complete Bible Commentary*, Grand Rapids, Kregel Publications, 1994, pg. 56.

CHAPTER 11

C.H. Mackintosh, *Notes on the Book of Exodus*, New York, Loizeaux Brothers, 1880, pg. 294.

CHAPTER 13

Arthur W. Pink, *Gleanings in Exodus*, Sovereign Grace Publishers, Lafayette, 2002, pg. 260.

CHAPTER 14

C.H. Mackintosh, *Notes on the Book of Leviticus*, New York, Loizeaux Brothers, 1880, pg. 181.

Albert Barnes, *Barnes' Notes on the New Testament*, Grand Rapids, Kregel Publications, 1966, pg. 272.

The Rev. Jimmy Swaggart is a Pentecostal evangelist whose anointed preaching and teaching has drawn multitudes to the Cross of Christ since 1956.

As an author, he has written more than 50 books, commentaries, study guides, and The Expositor's Study Bible, which has sold more than 1 million copies.

As an award-winning musician and singer, Brother Swaggart has recorded more than 50 Gospel albums and sold nearly 16 million recordings worldwide.

For nearly six decades, Brother Swaggart has channeled his preaching and music ministry through multiple media venues including print, radio, television and the Internet.

In 2010, Jimmy Swaggart Ministries launched its own cable channel, SonLife Broadcasting Network, which airs 24 hours a day to a potential viewing audience of more than 1 billion people around the globe.

Brother Swaggart also pastors Family Worship Center in Baton Rouge, Louisiana, the church home and headquarters of Jimmy Swaggart Ministries.

Jimmy Swaggart Ministries materials can be found at **www.jsm.org**.

NOTES

NOTES

NOTES

NOTES